MW00585645

THE CIO's GUIDE TO

BREAKTHROUGH

PROJECT PORTFOLIO PERFORMANCE

Applying the Best of Critical Chain, Agile, and Lean

MICHAEL HANNAN

WOLFRAM MÜLLER

HILBERT ROBINSON

First Printing: 2014

www.FortezzaConsulting.com

This title is available on www.Amazon.com and www.BookLocker.com. Bulk discounts are available for corporations, associations, libraries, educators, and others through www.BookLocker.com.

Special promotions may be offered by the publisher from time to time—consult www.FortezzaConsulting.com for current promotions.

ISBN 978-1-63443-943-5 (hard cover)
ISBN 978-1-63443-942-8 (paperback)

ISBNs listed in Books in Print under Primedia E-launch LLC

Printed in the United States of America

Dedication

For Krista, Carlos, Pablo, and José

Contents

Acknowledgments v

Purpose of this Book vii

Chapter 1: The Three Most Important Objectives.................1

    Project Selection.. 4
    Portfolio Throughput and Reliability 5

Chapter 2: How to Select the Right Projects 11

    Factoring in Investment... 19
    Incorporating Strategic Value....................................... 22
    IT Projects That Expand Capacity at the Constraint 23
    Special Consideration: When IT Is The System Constraint....... 24

Chapter 3: How to Maximize Portfolio Throughput..........29

    Project Staggering... 30
    Focused, Single-Task Execution 36
    Elimination of Task- or Sprint-level Commitments................... 42
    Lean Process Value Stream Analysis (VSA)................... 49
    Ultimate Scrum... 56
    Summary 68

Chapter 4: How to Optimize Portfolio Reliability 69

    Buffering.. 70
    Balancing Buffers Across the Project Portfolio 72
    Reliability Benefits of Focused, Single-Task Execution 76
    Reliability Benefits of Eliminating Task-level Commitments...78
    Reliability Benefits of Software-enabling Lean Processes 81
    Summary 81

Chapter 5: Fight the Zealotry 83

   Examples of Misplaced Zealotry...84
   Summary...91

Chapter 6: The Best of Both Worlds 93

   Buffer Balancing: The Integration Touch Point............................94
   Focused Execution 98
   Aggregated Risk..99
   Summary...100

Chapter 7: Putting It All Together 103

Chapter 8: Overcoming Obstacles 111

Chapter 9: How to Get Started 123

   Recommended Sequence of Technique Adoption.....................124
   Characteristics of an Ideal Large-scale Pilot...............................128

Appendix: When to Use Agile, and When Not to A-1

List of Tables and Figures

Table 1: Project Selection Considering Profit 17
Table 2: Project Selection Considering Profit Per Constraint
Unit 18
Table 3: Project Selection Considering "Effective ROI".......20

Figure 1: Typical Flow Density Chart 31
Figure 2: Throughput Benefits of Project Staggering..........34
Figure 3: Throughput Benefits of Single-Task Execution...41
Figure 4: Speed Benefits of Project-level Buffering 45

Figure 5: Throughput Benefits of Eliminating Task-level Commitments..48

Figure 6: Typical Examples of Non-Value-Added Steps 54

Figure 7: Throughput Benefits of Lean Process VSAs.........55

Figure 8: Drum-Buffer-Rope in Ultimate Scrum..................59

Figure 9: Cumulative Flow Diagram 61

Figure 10: End-to-end Ultimate Scrum Process....................65

Figure 11: Monitoring Project Progress Against Buffer Consumption 66

Figure 12: Throughput Benefits of Ultimate Scrum.............67

Figure 13: Balancing Project Buffers to Maximize Reliability 73

Figure 14: "Fever Chart" View of Balancing Buffers to Maximize Reliability 74

Figure 15: Fever Chart View of a Typical Project Portfolio Using BPI..75

Figure 16: Reliability Benefits of Focused, Single-Task Execution 77

Figure 17: Reliability Benefits of Aggregating Risk 79

Figure 18: Reliability Benefits of Project-level vs. Task-level Buffering..80

Figure 19: Showing All Three Buffer Types as Time-based95

Figure 20: Portfolio View of BPI by Buffer Type..................97

Figure 21: The Nine Techniques, Their Origins, and Primary Purpose 103

Figure 22: Task-level View 106

Figure 23: Project-level View 106

Figure 24: Portfolio-level View 107

Figure 25: View of All Levels Combined 108

Figure 26: Decision Tree for When to Use Agile and Lean Process VSAs... A-3

Acknowledgments

We would like to thank Roy Maizel, who gave Mike his first opportunity in program and project management at NASA, and all of the wonderful people at NOVACES who have supported Mike and Hilbert over the past few years. We also acknowledge Laura Barnard and Kendall Lott for all manner of advice and support surrounding the ideas in this book. And, finally, thanks to Maureen Hannan for her expert copy-editing.

Purpose of this Book

Our driving passion is helping organizations achieve breakthrough improvements in the performance of their project portfolios. For this book, we focus that passion on the uniquely wonderful challenges and opportunities inherent in information technology (IT) project portfolios.

The failure rate of IT projects has remained stubbornly high, in spite of a host of methods offering promise of relief—to the point that very few project stakeholders actually expect IT project portfolios to deliver a high volume of reliable project completions. And even when we do find ways to deliver some IT projects faster and more reliably, that success has proved difficult to replicate across the portfolio. "One-size-fits-all" approaches—such as mandating that all projects adopt Agile—often produce a hit-or-miss track record, leaving chief executives scratching their heads wondering why some projects realize great success, while others do not.

Exacerbating these throughput and reliability problems is the general sense that many projects in our portfolios, even when they come in as planned, fail to deliver anywhere close to the level of organizational benefit originally envisioned. Sometimes this is because of over-inflated promises made in order to obtain approval, but the more fundamental root cause is simply that most organizations have misguided project selection processes.

When we talk about breakthrough portfolio-wide improvements, we mean selecting much higher-impact projects, at least *doubling* the number of them that your organization can complete, and being able to deliver *over 90 percent* of them within plan—all within existing resource constraints. For profit-seeking enterprises, this translates to an effective return on investment (ROI) that is at least five times current levels, which in turn can multiply project-driven profits by 10X or better. For organizations measuring impact in terms other than profit, the breakthrough potential is commensurate.

As you might expect, achieving such dramatic results requires big changes—in how we work, in how we manage work, in our organizational values, and in how we foster unity of purpose at all levels and build trust with all internal and external stakeholders. But we have demonstrated that it can be done, and this book will show you how to do it.

Chapter 1: The Three Most Important Objectives

The three most important objectives for any project portfolio are

1) Selecting the right projects.
2) Maximizing the portfolio's throughput of project completions.
3) Optimizing the portfolio's reliability of project completions.

To many CIOs and IT project portfolio management (PPM) practitioners, focusing on these three objectives might seem obvious—of course we all want to pick high-impact projects and deliver a healthy volume of them reliably. The problem is that most of us haven't quite figured out how to do it.

Just how bad is this problem? The Project Management Institute (PMI) does an annual survey of over 2,500 project-management leaders and practitioners from all over the world, and asks them to assess their organizations' project-management performance.[1] Here are a few of the more telling metrics from the most recent survey:

- **Project selection:** Only 42 percent of projects were classified as having "high alignment" to organizational strategy.

- **Portfolio throughput:** Only 9 percent of respondents consider their organizations "excellent" at executing their highest-priority projects.

- **Portfolio reliability:** Only 17 percent of respondents believe that their organizations are able to realize envisioned project benefits with "high maturity."

Compounding this sad state of affairs is that most PPM solution approaches focus on only a part of the problem, or on addressing symptoms. For example, because portfolio reliability is so poor, projects going over budget must either siphon funds from other projects, or be killed or de-scoped to free up funds for

---

[1] *PMI's Pulse of the Profession: The High Cost of Low Performance*, 2014 (available free of charge at www.pmi.org/pulse).

other over-budget projects. As a result, the focus drifts from the root problem of poor reliability towards coming up with better approaches for deciding which projects to kill.

It's gotten so bad that even some of the largest-scale, most visible attempts to improve the performance of IT project portfolios fail to even mention throughput or reliability, while pointing to "savings" from killing or drastically de-scoping worthwhile projects. For example, the U.S. Federal Government launched an effort in 2010 to help improve the performance of its $60 billion-per-year IT project portfolio. A year later, the Federal CIO proudly cited almost $1 billion in cost reductions achieved, which sounds like a pretty good start. However, it turns out that nearly half of these cost reductions resulted from one-time data-center consolidations, and about a third came from terminating, halting, or de-scoping projects. Just $30M of the savings, a mere 0.5 percent of the Federal IT project portfolio, was attributed to "accelerated delivery."

We've seen similar patterns in dozens of IT project portfolios, across many major industries, all over the U.S., Europe, and Asia. The problem is large and pervasive, so we'll start by assessing each of the three primary objectives in turn. The chapters that follow will then provide specific guidance, techniques, and approaches for how to improve each of them.

Project Selection

While the PMI survey mentioned previously reveals poor project selection across many project-centric industries, many IT executives we speak with maintain that their project-selection processes are at least adequate. They say things like, "Project selection isn't rocket science—there are always mandatory initiatives to address security or compliance requirements; there is almost always at least one critical modernization initiative that should have been tackled years ago; there is usually a meaningful number of projects directly aligned with the CEO's strategic initiatives; and if there's any funding left over, it's not all that hard for each business unit to identify and advocate for its own top-priority initiatives."

In some ways, these statements resonate with us. After all, IT has become so critical to so many aspects of organizational performance, it seems there's no shortage of "must-do" projects—so maybe it's not so hard to pick the right projects if the only ones that fit within budget constraints are the must-do's. But if this logic were sound, we wouldn't see so many instances of IT project portfolios that fail to enable or improve our organizations' most critical business processes.

To cite one of the more sobering examples, the U.S. Department of Veterans Affairs' IT project portfolio has now grown to about $4 billion annually; yet 400,000 veterans' disability claims remain stuck in a queue for more than four months, and the IT system that manages the scheduling of patient visits recently showed 57,000 veterans waiting more than three months for a first appointment—so long, that some veterans *died* waiting. Of course, multiple factors contribute to such poor performance, well beyond inadequate IT project selection, but when such generously funded IT project portfolios fail to improve processes that are so central to the organization's mission, we must conclude that poor IT project selection remains a significant part of the problem.

Portfolio Throughput and Reliability

Once the right projects are selected, we then look at how well the portfolio executes them—specifically, how well the portfolio maximizes the throughput of project completions, while optimizing the percentage of projects that are delivered within planning constraints (scope, schedule, and budget). Because the throughput and reliability of project completions are often closely related, we will address them in tandem in this introductory chapter.

The PMI survey mentioned previously posted some bleak metrics on throughput and reliability; and given that these are measures of planning and execution performance, let's look first at the IT profession's most prevalent efforts to address project planning and execution. Two of these are the CMMI Institute's Capability Maturity Model Integration (CMMI), and PMI's similarly pervasive Project Management Body of Knowledge (PMBOK) and associated standards and certifications. CMMI focuses on improving the underlying processes required for successful IT project delivery, while PMI provides a set of foundational and "generally recognized good practices" that it reinforces via its certifications.

It would be logical to presume that using CMMI to improve IT project processes, and using PMI standards to promote good project practices, would result in improved throughput and reliability for IT project portfolios. As the PMI's own survey indicates, however, this is not often the case—and there are at least two primary reasons why. First, there is no mention of portfolio throughput or reliability in either CMMI or the PMBOK (or even in PMI's Standard for

Portfolio Management), let alone a maturity model to guide their improvement. Second, there is significant emphasis on what we would consider "input metrics"—such as repeatable processes and practices—without corresponding outcome metrics to assess whether this repeatability actually helps improve throughput or reliability.

To be fair, neither the CMMI Institute nor PMI claim to offer a specific set of methods or techniques for achieving a targeted set of results, and both would likely agree that any disciplined approach that helps improve the performance of IT project portfolios is welcome. Our purpose in mentioning them is not to criticize, but to make the point that, if your goal is to improve portfolio throughput and reliability, you will need to do more than achieve a certain CMMI-DEV maturity level or adhere to PMI's PMBOK and associated standards.

Agile represents another increasingly widespread attempt at improving the planning and execution of IT projects, and is arguably the most successful to date. If you have adopted Agile methods with any success in your IT project portfolio, you might reasonably point to improvements in throughput and reliability, and we commend you for achieving results that have eluded so many of your peers. Too often, however, Agile successes are isolated on just a few projects, or seem to follow a puzzling "hit-or-miss" pattern of impressive results on some projects, and minimal improvements on others. In addition, far too many attempts to scale Agile to every project in the portfolio have failed to deliver the dramatic improvements sometimes experienced at the project level. In some cases, the failure of "scaled" Agile adoption has been so visible and so complete that Agile is abandoned completely. This is unfortunate—we believe that Agile can play an important role in helping to improve the performance of IT project portfolios, but not without some adjustments, and only when placed into a disciplined portfolio management construct designed to maximize throughput and reliability.

To many Agile zealots, this may sound like heresy. "Adjustments? No need to fix something that ain't broke!" "Disciplined management construct? Agile works because it's self-managing!" We understand where this passion comes from, and while we enthusiastically embrace Agile and its contributions to throughput and reliability improvements, we cannot yet declare victory. The IT world remains plagued with failing project portfolios—including those with Agile projects—and too many smart, capable professionals

are set up for failure. What's desperately needed is a
practical mix of proven techniques and approaches,
blended harmoniously into a simple, coherent, "best-
tool-for-the-job" framework.

Chapter 2: How to Select the Right Projects

Let's start by looking at a reasonably mature project selection process that closely resembles many that we've come across:

1) **Project Identification**—Communicate the organizational strategy, and then ask each business unit to submit its top 10 project candidates, along with summary descriptions that include level of alignment with strategy, and some cost/benefit info for each.

2) **Project Validation**—Perform some high-level validation of the full list of project candidates, throwing out those candidates that don't meet minimum criteria, that seem only minimally compelling to the business as a whole, or that lack the strong political backing necessary to be considered seriously.

3) **Project Prioritization**—Convene an investment review board (IRB) comprised of top-echelon executives from across the organization, and have the IRB rack and stack the project candidates and

place them in priority order, using a weighted-criteria ranking approach.

4) **Project Selection**—Draw a line below the lowest-priority project candidate that still fits within the overall PMO budget, fund all projects above that line, and list the remaining below-the-line projects as "future candidates" (or just remove them from consideration altogether).

5) **Portfolio Politicking**—This has been going on the entire time, of course, but often gets particularly intense just before decisions are locked in. Watch the political wheeling and dealing kick into high gear, resulting in a "political peanut-butter spread" that avoids favoring or neglecting any business unit excessively, but makes sure to take special care of the most powerful business units.

There's a lot to like about this project selection process—it shows some discipline and alignment with organizational priorities, it fits within budget constraints, it's inclusive and tries to be fair, and it's flexible enough to bend to political realities. You might even wish your PMO's project selection process was as good as this one. However, it's also almost guaranteed to give the organization a mish-mash of middling results.

A real-world example might help illustrate why. One of the authors (Mike) had a client whose IT project selection process looked a lot like this—it had taken a lot of leadership initiative and trial-and-error to mature their process to this level, and they were justifiably proud of how far they'd come. Whereas not much of a process at all had been in place previously—they essentially just had Step 5 (the political wheeling and dealing)—now they could claim a mature, functional project selection process.

To their surprise, however, this new process resulted in an IT project portfolio that delivered essentially the same benefits and ROI as the old process. They asked Mike to take a look at their list of newly approved projects, and offer any insights he might have on ways to boost ROI. The list looked reasonable enough, and Mike couldn't take much issue with the merits of any project in particular. So he began by asking a simple question:

Mike: "What projects have the greatest potential to deliver the highest impact to overall organizational performance?"

Client: "I'd say Projects 1, 2, and 3...the ones that made it to the top of the priority list."

Mike: "OK, but Project 1 is for Business Unit 1, Project 2 is for Business Unit 2, and Project 3 is for Business Unit 3. Are there any projects that have the potential to deliver high impact to multiple business units?"

Client: "Yes, we have a few infrastructure upgrade projects that will benefit all business units, and a few projects that were actually proposed jointly by multiple business units."

Mike: "OK, but if you could point to a single business process that, if significantly improved, might deliver enormous benefit to the entire business, what would that business process be?"

Client: "Well, that would have to be the procurement process—we contract out a large portion of our budget, so any improvement in procurement would have immediate impact everywhere, and in a way that is central to our mission. But no one wants to touch procurement, because of all the complex regulatory requirements and mystifying legal issues—in fact, we've tried to improve procurement processes in the past, and gotten nowhere. Plus, our head of procurement has no real power base—it's the revenue-generating business units that have the power around here, not cost centers like procurement. And on top of all that, the head of procurement isn't a believer in IT, and hasn't even submitted any project proposals for consideration."

Mike: "OK, so you're saying that delivering high-impact results requires dealing with complexity, succeeding where others have failed, overcoming political hurdles, and taking leadership initiative when others won't?"

Client: "Point taken—OK, so how do we improve our project selection process?"

Our purpose in sharing this story is to show that, even with a mature project selection process, organizations often miss high-impact project candidates. In addition, this process lacks the discipline necessary to rank candidates according to their true ability to drive dramatic improvement in overall business performance. In the above story, it was obvious where such improvement was possible, but whether obvious or not, there is a discipline to identifying such high-impact processes.

This discipline comes from the Theory of Constraints (TOC), and its logic is straightforward: In any system, there is one function, resource, process area, or process step that constrains the entire system's ability to deliver on its mission. In the above story, that constraint is procurement. Once an organization has identified its system constraint, it knows that any improvement anywhere other than at the constraint will have little or no impact on overall organizational effectiveness. Putting this concept into practice helps provide much-needed clarity on where to focus improvement efforts.

Let's provide a more concrete example to demonstrate how to apply this TOC logic. Imagine that we have three software-development projects that we're trying to choose between, and that once the projects are complete and the software is put into operation, we've estimated the following expected revenues and costs:

Table 1: Project Selection Considering Profit

	Project X	Project Y	Project Z
Additional revenue per month	$90,000	$90,000	$100,000
Additional cost per month[2]	$45,000	$45,000	$40,000
Additional profit per month	$45,000	$45,000	$60,000

At first glance, it seems clear that Project Z is the best option of the three—it has both the highest revenue expectation, and the lowest expected cost. However, we have yet to factor in our system constraint—what if we only have 30 days' worth of work hours per month at our constraint to devote to whatever mix of projects is selected? In that case, Project Z uses up all available "constraint units," and delivers a monthly profit per constraint unit of $60,000. Projects X and Y are both lower profit per month ($45K each), but each requires only half of the available constraint units, affording us the option to choose both of them in lieu of Project Z. The result is a monthly profit of $90,000, or *50 percent*

---

[2] This consists of total variable cost, plus the fully amortized total project investment cost.

higher than Project Z. Even if we were to double our available constraint units, we will want to fund as many project candidates like X and Y as we can, before it makes sense for us even to consider Z.

Table 2: Project Selection Considering Profit Per Constraint Unit

	Project X	Project Y	Project Z
Days of constraint time required per month	15 days	15 days	30 days
Additional monthly profit (throughput[3]), per month of constraint time	$90,000	$90,000	$60,000

For organizations that do not measure their mission success in profit dollars, we can substitute whatever metric makes the most sense, and the approach works the same. So, whether we want to measure the throughput of profit dollars, or the throughput of

---

[3] Note that we are equating "additional monthly profit" with "throughput." This is because we are assuming that any operating expense is incorporated into total variable cost.

veterans receiving quality medical care, we can just use the term 'throughput' to cover all bases.[4]

This gives us a simple formula to start with:

Throughput per Constraint Unit (T/CU).

One way to think of T/CU is in terms of "effective throughput," as it represents what we actually expect to achieve, given what we know about how our system constraint limits throughput.[5] I simply need to get defensible estimates of T/CU for each project candidate, and fund the highest-scoring ones for which I have budget and available CUs to support.

Factoring in Investment

For simplicity, the above example assumes that all project investment funds are fully amortized into total variable cost. While this is becoming more of an option through software-as-a-service (SaaS) offerings, most IT project portfolios require a substantial pool of

---

[4] Not to be confused with "project throughput," which we use throughout this book to indicate the rate at which projects are completed.

[5] Effective throughput is sometimes referred to as "octane level" in TOC literature.

investment funds. As a result, we must incorporate investment into our project-selection model.

Table 3: Project Selection Considering "Effective ROI"

	Project X	Project Y	Project Z
Additional revenue per month	$90,000	$90,000	$100,000
Additional cost per month (total variable cost)	$30,000	$30,000	$30,000
Additional profit per month (throughput)	$60,000	$60,000	$70,000
Days of constraint time required per month	15 days	15 days	30 days
Additional monthly profit (throughput), per month of constraint time (T/CU)	$120,000	$120,000	$70,000
Total investment required to deliver project into operation	$900,000	$900,000	$600,000
Expected life-span of software system	5 years	5 years	5 years
Return on Investment (ROI) over life-span of software system	$3.6M/$90 0K, or 4x	$3.6M/$9 00K, or 4x	$4.2M/$60 0K, or 7x
T/CU per $1,000 invested	133	133	117

We've kept expected revenue and days of constraint time the same for all three projects, but moved the portion of total variable cost that was amortized investment down to the "total investment" line, in a single lump sum, and deliberately showed Projects X and Y as requiring significantly higher investment levels than Project Z. Keeping the expected life span for all three IT systems the same (five years), we then calculate the new monthly profit (throughput) figures that result, as well as the ROI and "T/CU per $1,000 invested" metrics.

As before, Project Z looks like the best project when considering its profitability, the smaller investment level required to fund the project, and the resulting high ROI. However, when considering Effective Throughput (T/CU) per dollar amount invested, Projects X and Y still score higher. We now have a somewhat improved project-selection metric that we'll call "Effective ROI," as it calculates the actual ROI expected when taking into account the system constraint:[6]

---

[6] Note that T/CU/I is mathematically equivalent to T/I/CU. For those readers familiar with the notion of "investment turns," T/I is the throughput accounting formula for investment turns, so T/I/CU can also be thought of as "investment turns per constraint unit."

To be even more accurate, we would need to refine the metric further by factoring in how long those investment dollars are tied up in project work, and incorporating the time value of money for the entire model. However, try to resist the temptation to over-engineer these calculations, as you will very quickly see the "law of diminishing returns" come into play.

Incorporating Strategic Value

While Effective ROI provides a focused method for high-impact project selection, strategic considerations should often be factored in as well. For example, some IT projects are designed to help improve brand awareness, test out the effectiveness of a new marketing campaign or new solution offering, gain market share, build customer loyalty, and so on. In order to promote a consistent "apples-to-apples" framework for assessing competing project candidates, we must convert any "strategic value" component into a rough equivalent of revenue. In addition, if there are any "non-dollar costs" such as the risk of harming brand value, losing market share, or alienating customers, these should be factored in as well—either by deflating the converted revenue figure, or by inflating the total variable cost figure.

Some of our clients have also stressed the importance of showing a variety of "portfolio views" of their candidate projects, to depict the spread of candidate projects across business units, or the mix of strategic vs. profit-making projects, or the mix of candidate projects by product line. These are fine—our only words of caution are to make sure these breakouts don't lead you into stovepipe thinking and practices. In other words, never lose the discipline of examining the entire portfolio of candidate projects according to Effective ROI.

IT Projects That Expand Capacity at the Constraint

Typically, the first few IT projects that go into production operation can take full advantage of available CUs, especially as the organization learns to expose hidden capacity by focusing all efforts on maximizing throughput at the constraint. At some point, however, most or all of this hidden capacity will get used up, such that any further projects delivering new capabilities into operation will only serve to overload the constraint, degrading throughput. As a result, the only projects that make sense at that point are those that can actually expand capacity at the constraint. Note that our T/CU/I formula still applies, but it is critical that the organization understand which projects are designed to exploit available CUs, and which are designed to expand CUs—and then sequence projects accordingly.

Special Consideration: When IT Is The System Constraint

For many organizations, IT has become so critical to so many facets of the organization, that IT itself has become the system constraint. Sometimes the problem may manifest itself as the entire function of IT constraining overall organizational throughput, but more often it's focused on a select few IT staff resources—typically senior technical architects or developers, expert on multiple critical IT systems and technologies, who are also highly effective troubleshooters. To personify this resource type, let's call her "Susan" (though there may well be more than just one "Susan"). Beyond the management challenges of how to avoid spreading Susan too thin, how to avoid multi-tasking her, and how to focus her on key organizational priorities (addressed in Chapters 3 and 4), this scenario presents some tricky problems for project selection.

As an example, consider the following. We have a candidate software-development project that ranks first in Effective ROI, and once delivered into production operation, will require a substantial level of constraint time from Susan. In addition, it turns out that the project itself also requires considerable time from Susan. If this project is the first one in the queue, these demands may present no issue at all, as Susan first works the project to completion, and then devotes her time as "constraint unit" once the software system goes into operation. But what about all ensuing projects? Their Effective ROI must take into account that the available constraint units (Susan) will be far less available for their operations once Project #1 goes live. Magnify this problem further once Project #2, #3, #4, and so on all enter the picture: All will require more of Susan, both for development and for operation. If the projects are not managed well, the result will be that the organization will nearly grind itself to a halt. Project work and operations work will both find that there just aren't enough Susans to go around. All original estimates of T/CU/I end up way off in the midst of this compounded CU shortage, projects take significantly longer than initially estimated, and operational effectiveness is severely degraded.

The solution to this problem has three parts:

1) **Keep Susan focused.** Protect her from ad-hoc tasking, while maximizing single-task focus that is aligned with organizational priorities. Make clear that her priority is no longer responding to fires, but staying focused on executing the assigned task at hand. Schedule her resource to take on project tasks according to a given number of available hours per day or per week, and operations tasks for the remainder of her time.

2) **Subordinate all other resources to Susan.** In other words, all resources other than Susan (non-CUs) must do whatever they can to help alleviate the pressure on Susan. Even minor assistance can have a big impact—we've even seen examples of organizations asking non-CUs to go bring Susan her lunch so she can maximize her available CU time. Even better is when non-CUs shadow Susan and document some of her more repeatable approaches, such as how best to troubleshoot a particular system; oftentimes, the non-CUs even find ways to automate or simplify these approaches, further freeing up Susan.

3) **Generate more Susans**. While this may well
   take more time and effort—and will likely
   require even more of Susan's CUs initially—it
   simply must be done. For example, there must
   be deliberate efforts to have non-CUs pick up
   knowledge or skills that only Susan currently
   has, such as gaining expertise in a critical
   operational system that Susan knows really
   well.

Note that these steps should be taken whether IT is the
constraint or not. When IT is the constraint, make sure
to maintain project-selection discipline, even in the
face of major capacity issues, and even if those
capacity issues drive down the volume of approved
projects in the near term. Stay as true to Effective ROI
as you can, being appropriately conservative on CU
estimates when IT (or Susan) represents both the
scarce project resource and the operational constraint.

A critically important final point on this: If you can
find a way to get more projects done without adding
resources, you will have a greater ability both to
expand capacity at the constraint, and to use that
additional capacity to drive up throughput. The next
chapter focuses on how to do exactly that.

Chapter 3: How to Maximize Portfolio Throughput

When we say "portfolio throughput," we are specifically referring to how many project completions an organization can achieve over a given period of time. If we think of the organization's total set of project portfolio resources as a busy stretch of highway, and we think of projects as flowing through the organization like people traveling on that highway, then maximizing portfolio throughput would be equivalent to maximizing how many people we can have travel that stretch of highway over a given period of time.

We can boost highway throughput in a number of ways—here are some common ones:

- We can keep the road free of impediments and in good working order.
- We can increase traffic density (e.g., carpooling).
- We can meter the on-ramps whenever their inflow slows the main flow of traffic.
- We can recruit underutilized resources elsewhere (such as lanes usually devoted to opposing traffic).

- We can try and make the cars go faster.
- We can build an additional a lane or two.

In PPM, we tend to focus mostly on trying to make the cars go faster—even when the highway is all jammed up, sometimes causing accidents, and usually frustrating everyone on the highway who can't get where they want to go. We also tend to jump right to trying to add a lane or two—which is rarely quick, easy, or inexpensive, if it's a feasible option at all.

So, while speed is important, and adding capacity may well be in order, let's start by getting traffic to flow. Step 1 is already done—we've improved project selection, so that we only have the right travelers on the highway to begin with. However, if we throw them into traffic all at the same time using the same on-ramp, we will likely just create a traffic jam. So we need to meter the flow of on-ramp traffic in a way that keeps highway traffic flowing. In the PPM world, we call this project staggering.

Project Staggering

As with the highway analogy, project staggering is based on the concept of "flow density." As shown in the flow-density graphic below, the first person to enter the highway will go as fast as he wants, but if all we have is that single individual, our flow is obviously very low. If we add a second person, we double the flow instantly, as there is still plenty of room to go as fast as both people care to. We can keep adding more people, one at a time, and the flow will rise accordingly, until we hit a certain density, at which point our flow improvements start to taper. If we keep adding more travelers, we will hit a point at which our flow peaks, and then starts to degrade. If we continue to push more cars onto the highway, we will worsen the flow dramatically, until our density is so high that we have very little flow at all.

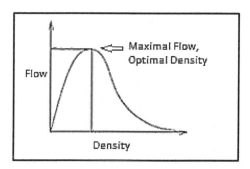

Figure 1: Typical Flow Density Chart

The same holds true for projects flowing through an organization. The primary difference is that, with a highway, it's easier to see the available capacity (lanes) and the flow (cars driving by). In PPM, how can I visualize my organization's total project capacity? If I just finished five medium-sized projects, does that mean I now have the capacity to kick off five new ones; or was I already too far down the flow density curve? Do the five new projects require more of a scarce resource, or less? And even if they require less, might they all require that resource at the same time?

In order to visualize an organization's PPM capacity, we obviously need to be able to answer some basic questions about our resource pool, such as, "How many senior systems architects do we have, and how well utilized are they currently?" But we must also have good insight into the timing for which each project resource will be needed, and understand where my biggest resource constraints actually lie. The only way to know these things for sure is to have all projects planned out, with tasks and task dependencies identified, and task resources assigned. In our experience, however, you can begin to get a pretty good idea of where the resource bottlenecks are likely to occur, as they tend to follow a pattern in IT projects.

Specifically, the early phases of concept refinement and solution architecture tend to require seasoned, highly skilled staff, as do integration tasks in later phases. So as long as you have a reasonably good idea for how to avoid having these phases across projects bump into each other, you are ready to stagger your projects. In the highway example, this is done by allocating a slice of resource availability (space in a lane); the same goes for IT PPM, except that this resource is usually an individual or a team.

Figure 2 provides an example of staggering for a simple project portfolio, executed by three resources (A, B, and C). Without staggering, we can see that portfolio throughput is three projects over 17 weeks. This example assumes that all projects are kicked off at roughly the same time, and that resources are spread across all projects. With staggering, we see that all three projects finish four to eight weeks earlier, even though the third project isn't even kicked off until Week 7. We also see that staggering gives us the ability to deliver four projects in less time than delivering three using a simultaneous execution approach.

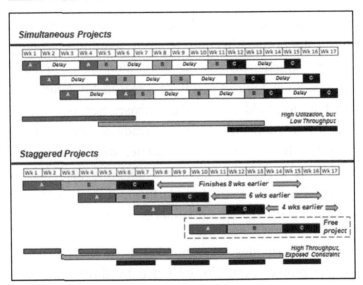

Figure 2: Throughput Benefits of Project Staggering

In addition to improving the throughput of project completions significantly, we have also exposed the resource that is limiting further throughput improvements—specifically, "Resource B." In other words, if we can add just a little more Resource B, or can find ways to have Resources A or C help lighten the load of B, we might be able to deliver a fifth project within 17 weeks. In contrast, we can see more clearly that adding more Resource A or Resource C will not help me improve throughput at all.

So, in addition to helping us improve the throughput of project completions, project staggering has given us a very useful gift in exposing Resource B as our project portfolio's throughput constraint—we now know exactly where to focus our improvement efforts.

If you are an Agile practitioner, you might be tempted to conclude that the PPM example above looks suspiciously like an instance of a "waterfall" approach, and therefore not relevant to Agile projects. But all projects follow a logical sequence, with phases such as concept refinement taking place earlier, development occurring somewhere in the middle, and integration after that. So project staggering is agnostic on specific project-level methods.

This notion of "method-agnosticism" in project staggering is critically important. Many IT executives have been told that, in order to exploit Agile's speed and reliability benefits across their portfolios, the organization must adopt Agile on all projects. Agile-only PPM frameworks have sprung up to support this misguided notion. But while Agile has shown us that dramatic project-level improvements are possible, there are many ways to improve portfolio performance—including project staggering. And at the project level, Agile can help on certain types of projects—or just in some parts or phases of the project—but may not be the best approach for others.

(For more on this, see the Appendix: When to Use Agile, and When Not to).

For CIOs, IT Project Portfolio Managers, and other senior executives looking for a more practical, hybrid approach for improving the throughput of project completions, project staggering is your first step.

Focused, Single-Task Execution

How often have you heard people brag about what great multi-taskers they are? Perhaps you've made the same boast yourself. You might even have heard that members of "Gen Y" are natural multi-taskers, having lived their whole lives constantly switching their attention from texting to IMing to Facebooking to watching TV—all supposedly without missing a beat. We even see training classes designed to teach managers how best to multi-task their Gen Y staff, the implication being that asking someone to focus on a single task through to completion has now become ridiculously old-fashioned for, if not downright heretical to, the new world order.

Don't believe it. First of all, true multi-tasking is something human beings are only minimally capable of doing. Think in terms of juggling with one hand while brushing your teeth with the other. Sure, there are people who can train themselves to do both tasks simultaneously; but not many really can pull it off—and even fewer will do it well. And, in any case, such rare individuals are more likely to be found in a circus than in a typical office environment.

So psychologists and organizational-development specialists have begun to use the more accurate term "task switching" in lieu of "multi-tasking," arguing that task switching better describes the norm of Gen Y, and of the business world generally. Specifically, task switching refers to the interruption of a task in progress, for the purpose of picking up a separate task. Sounds like something we all deal with dozens of times a day, right? You might even be thinking, "Hey, that's just modern reality—either figure out a way to get good at it, or get left behind."

The truth, however, is that task switching is slowing us down a lot—by a whopping 40 percent, according to many studies.[7] Are we really surprised that constantly switching tasks causes such a huge productivity loss? After all, when we see focused execution in action, we

---

[7] See https://www.apa.org/research/action/multitask.aspx for a review of such studies.

can't help but marvel at how much faster it is. For instance, many of us put in an hour or two of work either early in the morning, or late at night, "because that's when I can really get things done." We know intuitively that we're much more productive when we're able to minimize interruptions and task switching.

Ever see someone solve a Rubik's Cube in less than 30 seconds? They're not task switching. Many software developers talk about how highly productive they are when they can eliminate all distractions and "get in the zone." In fact, the software industry came up with the Agile methodology and its "sprints," in part, to promote this type of focused execution on software-development projects.

Of course, just having your project's tasks time-boxed into a sprint doesn't, by itself, do anything to eliminate task switching. In fact, when you hear examples of Agile failures, it's a good bet that pervasive task switching was one of the main culprits. After all, it's relatively straightforward to time-box a set of tasks, but it takes real leadership to structure a work environment and foster a culture that together promote single-task focus as the desired norm.

Can you guess what industry has the most advanced, mature adoption of single-task focus?

Perhaps the software industry? Sure, some software companies achieve high productivity this way (and we've helped a few get there), but they are still the exception.

What about healthcare providers? They certainly have examples, such as an operating room or an exam room, in which single-task focus predominates, but most other aspects of healthcare delivery are plagued with task switching.

Maybe the military? Many operational aspects of warfare certainly promote single-tasking, and battle plans are often designed around focusing fighting units on a single objective. However, most military commanders would not characterize the real-world experience of fighting a battle as interruption-free; on the contrary, they emphasize the importance of "adapting and improvising," which sounds to us more like task switching than single-task execution.

The answer is the education industry. For centuries, the entire operational model of a school has been designed to promote focus on a single lesson at a time, through to completion. While there remains enormous room for improvement in education, and while some schools certainly adhere to single tasking better than others, it would be absurd to imagine any school in which the science teacher rushed into math class mid-period, interrupted the math lesson with a science lesson, and then rushed back out without even finishing the science lesson.

Yet we have come to view this absurdity as normal—even desirable—in our project environments and in the business world generally. We have somehow convinced ourselves that it's just the way things are—that there's nothing we can do about it, even if we wanted do. Yet, when we're confronted with examples as commonplace as a classroom, we see that it's not really so rare, and hardly an advanced management-science concept.

Consider one more illustration of how focused, single-task execution can contribute to the throughput of project completions. If you recall from our project-staggering example earlier in this chapter, we boosted our throughput from three projects to four projects, with an idea or two for raising it to five projects. Assuming that most or all of our projects suffer from pervasive task-switching, we would expect an average productivity benefit of 40 percent from focused, single-task execution. Let's, however, be a bit more conservative than that, and assume a 35-percent gain. (We know that's still a lot, but we've seen some organizations benefit more than that, and in any case, we want to give you a sense of just how much improvement is realistically possible.)

As shown in the example, a 35-percent gain in productivity from focused, single-task execution would jack up throughput to seven project completions, compared to our original metric of just three. So if all we do is stagger our projects and execute them with

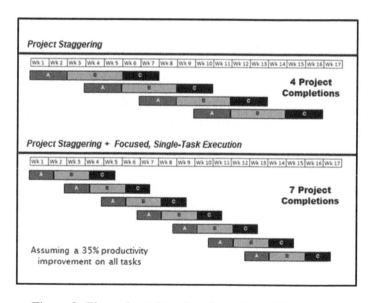

Figure 3: Throughput Benefits of Single-Task Execution

single-task focus, we can more than double portfolio throughput. But let's not stop there.

Elimination of Task- or Sprint-level Commitments

Project management and execution is a risky business. As a project manager or scrum master, our natural desire is to address this inherent risk by seeking out anything that we feel we can depend on, so we like it when our most dependable task leads or scrum teams commit to delivering on their tasks or sprints by a given date. What may not be obvious, however, is the price we pay for these reliable task/sprint completions in project-level speed and throughput.

An example might help illustrate this phenomenon. Imagine that you are a responsible task owner, and also a top performer who has demonstrated near-heroic ability to deliver on aggressive task durations. You are assigned a complex task that you are highly confident you can complete in 10 days. In fact, you have in the past delivered on similar tasks in as few as four days when everything went your way. Your PM asks you into her office to discuss what task duration you can commit to:

PM: "As you know, this project is under enormous schedule pressure—I need you to deliver on your usual heroics, and commit to the most aggressive task due date that you can."

You: "Okay—this is a complex one that I think would take your average performer at least 20 days, but I'm confident I can deliver on it in 10 days."

PM: "I wish I could give you 10 days, but I can't give you more than five. You and I both know you've performed miracles on similarly complex tasks in as few as four days, so I need you to commit to five days."

You: "Well, I'd say that there's only a 50/50 chance that I could meet that 5-day commitment. I've worked hard to establish a strong reputation as someone who delivers on his commitments, so while I welcome the challenge of delivering in five days or less, I simply cannot risk my reputation by committing to five days."

Conversations like this one tend to consume significant time and energy on projects, and they rarely resolve in a manner that fosters unity of purpose and trust-building between PM and Task Lead. If the Task Lead takes the risk and fails, he will be extra-vigilant about fighting for the 10-day duration next time; if he succeeds, the PM will be equally vigilant about imposing the 5-day duration next time, even though the risk of failure remains the same.

Either way, the risk of failure at five days is still 50/50, and so the reliability that both PM and Task Lead seek will almost invariably lead to the 10-day window. And once the 10-day window is established, the Task Lead would be highly unlikely ever to deliver earlier than that, for fear that the PM might force him to commit to that more aggressive timeline going forward.

To see how this negatively affects project throughput, let's use our example of the 10-day vs. the 5-day task, and further assume that we have a total of four such tasks that must be delivered in sequential order with finish-to-start dependencies.

As depicted in Figure 4, using a 50/50 estimation method, we calculate a total of 20 days of work, on average. But it would be foolish to commit to 20 days, because that estimate leaves no buffers should anything go wrong and cause significant delays.

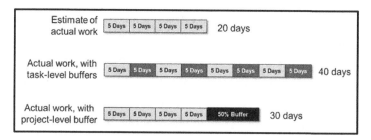

Figure 4: Speed Benefits of Project-level Buffering

So, one choice is to ask each of the four Task Leads to commit to 10 days, even though we know that they will all require some buffer on their task execution in order to commit. Another choice, however, is to hold all buffer at the project level, and challenge our Task Leads to deliver early, with the promise that they won't be held to any specific commitment at all. Once trust is established that this project-level buffer really will be there if any Task Lead needs it, this "aggregated risk" approach will require fewer overall buffer days than the costly "self-insurance" approach of task-level buffering, boosting our project speed from 40 days to 30 days, or 25 percent. As a result, there is no longer any benefit to asking for any task-level commitments at all.

This strategy goes against the established management practice of "holding people accountable," and thus deserves some additional discussion. If people aren't even asked to commit on a given task, won't they relax too much, slow down, and lose focus? It turns out that the answer is no—people, as a rule, enjoy being highly productive—and tend to have even higher motivation when they can manage their own pace of work. Especially in high-risk environments like projects, it actually helps build unity of purpose and trust when staff see that managers above them are assuming responsibility for project risk, and buffering the task-level risk as needed. The aggregated risk approach frees everyone from the need to have the "how aggressively can you commit?" conversation, and allows all team members to focus instead on how to be a high-performing team. And if certain team members decide to take advantage of the "no-commitment" approach by slowing things down, it won't take long for managers and other team members to notice it and take appropriate action.

The same principle holds true for Agile projects. If the scrum team commits to overly aggressive delivery on a given sprint, it won't take too many sprints before the team will fail to meet its commitment. Seeking to avoid developing a reputation as a team that fails to deliver on its commitments, the scrum team will act more responsibly going forward. They will self-insure against the risk of things going awry by committing only to a level of work product that they are confident they can deliver. So, as in the previous example, they sign up for less, and deliver less.

As with traditional projects, the better alternative is to aggregate the lower-level risk at the project level and just let the scrum team do its thing—breaking speed records on good sprints and slogging through bad sprints as best they can. As long as the project's "desirement sprints" are adequate to absorb the aggregated risks faced on all bad sprints, the project will deliver on its commitment—especially if the good sprints are exploited fully.

Interestingly, Agile's scrum-team approach has its own way of aggregating some execution risk. For example, in a traditional "single task owner" approach, the risk of execution is not aggregated at all, leaving that task owner to add a lot of task-level buffer to self-insure and deliver on his commitment. In contrast, a 5-person scrum team aggregates the risk that any single individual will make slow progress, as the other four team members can often make up the deficit.

But why aggregate only up to the scrum-team level? Taking a lesson from the insurance industry, the more that risk can be aggregated, the easier it is to manage.

Applied to projects, this will nearly always mean that it's better to aggregate risk at the project level. As a result, an Agile project can improve speed by avoiding sprint-level commitments.

Let's look at the impact that eliminating task- and sprint-level commitments can have on the portfolio's throughput of project completions. From the earlier example, we improved one project's duration from 40 days to 30 days, or 25 percent. Figure 5 depicts how this 25-percent speed improvement would translate into portfolio throughput.

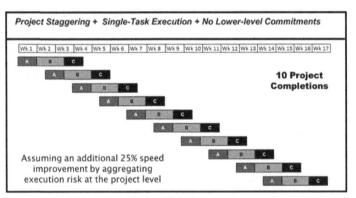

Figure 5: Throughput Benefits of Eliminating Task-level Commitments

Recall that we started at a throughput level of three projects over 17 weeks. By combining project staggering, single-task execution, and elimination of task/sprint-level commitments, we see that we can now *more than triple* portfolio throughput—and none of these techniques is complex or difficult to learn and apply.[8]

Thus far, everything we've covered can be applied to any type of project portfolio, whether IT, construction, engineering, R&D, or any other project-centric domain. We will now present additional throughput-improvement techniques that offer unique advantages to IT project portfolios—and especially to software-development projects.

Lean Process Value Stream Analysis (VSA)

The entire value proposition of software is based on its ability to improve business processes. But software engineering and process engineering are far more distinct than many of us realize. In fact, the two fields are often at odds with one another—software engineers often take the opinion that "drawing boxes and arrows" isn't really all that hard, while process engineers often wonder why so much software seems only to enable

---

[8] For those readers unfamiliar with Critical Chain Project Management (CCPM), you might be interested to know that these three techniques form CCPM's project-level foundation.

complex processes instead of simplifying them. Software engineers often seem to take the attitude, "Tell me your requirements, so that I can go develop software to implement them." Process engineers, on the other hand, would more likely say, "Tell me your process, so that I can help you engineer a way to make it significantly simpler, faster, and more reliable.

In short, the process engineers are right. Even the most prevalent software-engineering frameworks seem to gloss over the importance of leaning out processes before any software development takes place, and many software engineers seem to enjoy the challenge of enabling highly complex processes. They have the perfect excuse: "But the process owner insisted that this is the process they need us to enable!" Once you spend a little time with some top-notch process engineers, however, you quickly learn just how bloated most business processes are. Because complex processes = complex software, shrinking the process footprint of software-development projects helps tighten scope, enabling us to execute those projects more quickly, and increase our throughput of project completions.

For example, for a recent client, a number of competent software engineers from a well-regarded systems integrator dutifully mapped out 10-12 specific business processes for which the client's process owners requested software enablement. One of these processes addressed a moderately complex process area, calling for 523 steps. In response, one of us challenged the client to let a few of our process engineers simplify that process before expending significant software-development effort to enable it. The client agreed. One month later, the client's process owners released their new 22-step process, a *95-percent reduction* from the original 523 steps.

It turns out that this is higher than normal, but not by much—seasoned process engineers will tell you that the typical business process contains 70-90 percent bloat. The challenge is to devote time, energy, and the right talent into improving processes before software-enabling them.

This commitment to lean processes requires significant expertise—including the ability to educate process owners on what great processes look like, to show them what it takes to improve processes so dramatically, and to push back hard when they are reluctant to let go of wasteful steps. While many techniques from Lean, Six Sigma, and elsewhere can drive process improvement, the one most conducive to our PPM throughput-maximization objective is Lean's Process VSA. We will therefore focus in on that one here.

How Process VSAs Help

For our narrow purposes, the primary benefit of a Process VSA is the substantial net reduction of steps in a process—though we'll gladly accept other benefits that Process VSAs can deliver, such as process speed, reliability, simplicity, and transparency. If the process gurus are right, and 70-90 percent of most business processes consist of "non-value-added" steps, then eliminating them will help us slash our software-development effort.

In order to satisfy Lean's definition of a "value-added" step, that step must meet three conditions:

1) Change the object being moved through the process.
2) Deliver a result that's done right the first time.
3) Deliver value—as defined by the customer of that process.

In a commercial or fee-for-service setting, satisfying #3 can be as simple as seeing whether customers are willing to pay for the step. In practice, however, it is not always so clear-cut—since the customer of a given process may not be an actual paying end customer. For example, the customer of an internal payroll process could be an employee. There are also many examples of public-sector end customers who may not pay money for a process step, but who may pay in time and effort, such as a veteran seeking medical care at a veterans' hospital.

If a given step fails to meet all three of these conditions, it is considered non-value-added, and is a target for elimination. It may sometimes be necessary to simplify or otherwise improve steps elsewhere in the process before it makes sense to eliminate a non-value-added step. In addition, there may exist "non-value-added, but required" steps, such as those mandated by law. Figure 6 provides a few of the more typical examples of non-value-added steps.

▸ Steps that satisfy internal stakeholders, but which do little or nothing that the customer cares about ▸ Steps that consist of reviewing, approving, and reworking	*Eliminate*
▸ Steps that deliver low-quality results—which necessitate all the reviewing/approving/ reworking in the first place—are changed to deliver high-quality results	*Improve*
▸ Steps that call for complex branching and merging are replaced by simple "standard work" steps that are perfectly acceptable.	*Simplify*

Figure 6: Typical Examples of Non-Value-Added Steps

If we can eliminate 70-90 percent of the steps in a business process before software-enabling it, we could conceivably eliminate a similarly high percentage of the total software-development effort. While we would obviously need to factor in the time and effort required to shrink the process footprint in the first place, in our experience this time-and-effort investment usually comprises just a fraction of the expected benefit.

Let's take a look at how streamlining the process in this way would further improve our portfolio throughput performance. To be conservative, let's assume that the total net benefit from applying the Lean Process VSA for our software-development projects is only half of the 70-90 percent metric, or a

40-percent improvement. Let's further assume that only half of our IT project portfolio is comprised of software-development projects, and that no other type of IT project (e.g., infrastructure modernization) can benefit from a Process VSA. So our 40-percent improvement estimate is cut in half, to 20 percent—a very achievable estimate, in our experience.

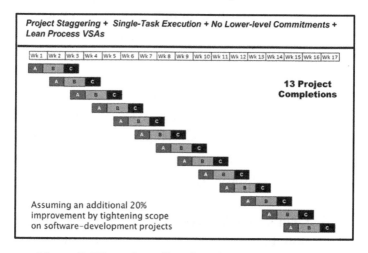

Figure 7: Throughput Benefits of Lean Process VSAs

As shown in Figure 7, by using these first four techniques in combination, we can now more than *quadruple* our portfolio's throughput of project completions—from three to thirteen in our simple portfolio example. But we're not done yet.

Ultimate Scrum[9]

The objective of Ultimate Scrum is to maximize the productive flow of software-development work. It does this using an innovative mix of proven techniques from Agile, Lean, and the Theory of Constraints (TOC) to drive up the throughput of task completions.

In addition to subscribing to many Agile/Scrum tenets, Ultimate Scrum takes its three flow-improving pillars from Lean and TOC:

1) Lean's "pull system," which drives flow more effectively than a "push system." In Ultimate Scrum, software developers pull their tasks from the backlog, as opposed to managers assigning (pushing) tasks.

2) Lean's "single-piece flow" as the ideal unit of flow in a high-performing process. In Ultimate Scrum, single-piece flow manifests as a rule that developers may pull only one task at a

---

[9] Ultimate Scrum was developed by co-author Wolfram Müller of Speed4Projects.net. Ultimate Scrum content in this book has appeared in previous works, including *Tame the Flow: Hyper-Productive Knowledge Work Management*, by Steve Tendon and Wolfram Müller, 2013, and is used with permission.

time, and that no developer may start a new task until finishing the one in progress.

3) TOC's tenet that the throughput of a system is maximized only when governed by the pace of that system's constraint. In Ultimate Scrum, the software developers are the constraint, and their velocity of task completion sets the pace for all supporting aspects of task flow.

While it is not the purpose of this book to delve into significant details on Lean and TOC, some discussion of these three pillars is in order. First, Lean's pull system is a demand-driven approach that promotes efficient flow by ensuring that the only items entering a process are those that process participants pull into it. This approach is highly consistent with the self-organizing nature of Agile, and many scrum teams have adopted pull systems to manage the flow of tasks.

Second, Lean's single-piece flow—also commonly referred to as "batch-size reduction"—is based on the concept that smaller batch sizes are easier to pull through a process than large batch sizes. A good analogy here is eating bite-size pieces of food rather than a huge mouthful. If the smallest batch size possible is 1, and achieving a batch size of 1 with minimal-to-zero processing overhead is feasible, then single-piece flow will be optimal.

An important side benefit of Agile's sprints is that they reduce the batch sizes of tasks, compared to most traditional approaches. Ultimate Scrum pushes this concept to the limit by achieving a batch size of 1, effectively doing away with sprints altogether, in favor of a single-piece flow of tasks. This is consistent with Little's Law, which holds that the lead time of in-process items (tasks) is proportional to the number of in-process items. In other words, the more open tasks you have, the longer the lead time to complete them, and the slower the process moves.

So if we minimize the number of open tasks, the process speeds up. Replacing the "task batching" of sprints with continuous, single-piece flow will therefore improve the speed of execution. Doing away with sprints in this fashion also means that you no longer need to spend valuable time in sprint reviews discussing half-finished stories.

Finally, Ultimate Scrum employs TOC's "Drum-Buffer-Rope" (DBR) method for maximizing the effective throughput of task completions as efficiently as possible. The **drum** refers to the developers, as they are the system constraint for software development, and thus set the pace or "drumbeat" of task execution. In order to make sure that the developers always have a ready supply of tasks, we make sure to **buffer** them with just enough open tasks in progress. And in order to know when we need to release a new open task to the buffer, we need to get a tug on the "**rope**," which in this case happens every time a task is finished.

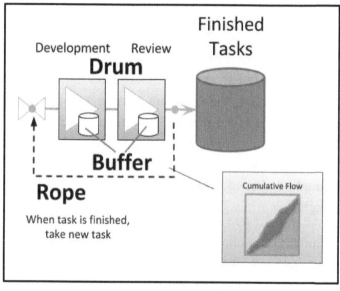

Figure 8: Drum-Buffer-Rope in Ultimate Scrum

When applying DBR to achieve maximum throughput with optimal efficiency, the only real challenge is determining the appropriate buffer size, or optimum number of open tasks. If there are too many open tasks, then Little's Law takes over and slows down lead times. If there are too few open tasks, then we risk allowing our developers to become idle—a problem we definitely want to avoid.[10]

If all developer tasks are always done independently by a single individual, then the optimal number of open tasks would be one per developer. However, because teams can sometimes achieve higher levels of productivity by working in small groups—such as performing code reviews on each other's work—there are times when two developers are working the same task. As a result, the optimum number of open tasks will always be fewer than the number of developers on the team. For example, if teamwork occurs 20 percent of the time and you have ten developers, then the optimal number of open tasks will be 10 − (20%)(10), or eight.

Optimizing the number of open tasks in this way results in a valuable side benefit as well. Specifically, the moment a developer hits a road block on her task,

---

[10] In TOC, allowing your system constraint to become idle is referred to as "starving the constraint."

she may not just put it aside unfinished and start on another one. Rather, the impediment is identified immediately, help from other team members is provided to resolve, and the solution for removing the impediment is captured for future use. The team learns to focus on maintaining the flow, and to resolve a greater volume of challenging issues on its own.

As shown in Figure 9, we use a Cumulative Flow Diagram (CFD) to monitor task throughput, lead times,

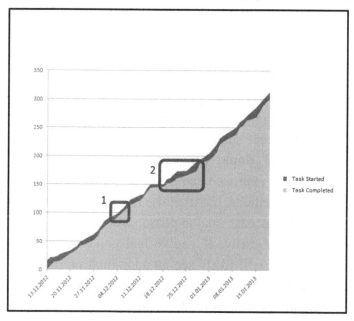

Figure 9: Cumulative Flow Diagram

and volume of tasks in process (often referred to as "inventory"). The objective is to maximize throughput (making the slope as steep as possible), while minimizing lead times and inventory (keeping the darker-shaded area as thin as possible).

The diagram shows Little's Law at work—in the area marked "1," we see quick lead times and very little inventory, whereas in the area marked "2" there are more tasks open and therefore slower flow times.

What About Kanban?

For those readers familiar with Kanban, you might be wondering why we propose using DBR in lieu of Kanban to govern the pace of task flow. Kanban is an increasingly popular Lean method to organize tasks into the three simple categories of **pending**, **in-process**, and **done**, across all major phases of a project. This approach can be a big improvement over traditional methods, but it allows more in-process tasks than DBR, at each major phase, which slows things down unnecessarily. If you've had good results with Kanban, you will likely see an additional productivity bump with DBR; if you're new to both Kanban and DBR, you might perceive Kanban as the more intuitive approach to grasp and implement, but we encourage you to give DBR a try—it has its own simple elegance for helping you pursue optimum performance, and many organizations have applied it with great success.

What About Other Agile/Scrum Techniques?

Given that we eliminated sprint commitments earlier in this chapter, and Ultimate Scrum calls for eliminating sprints altogether, you might be wondering what Agile/Scrum techniques remain. The answer is nearly all of them—daily standups, product backlogs, and retrospectives all remain intact, with burndown charts still useful as well. Reviews make sense too, but given that the sprints are gone, reviews can instead be conducted each time a story is finished (single-piece flow). Every 5-10 finished stories, it makes sense to package up finished work and show it to the Product Owner and other stakeholders.

What About Breaking User Stories into Tasks?

Up to this point, we've focused discussion of Ultimate Scrum on the part of the process that deals with software-development task execution. We will now address the upstream part of the process, in which we break user stories into features and tasks. Simply put, the goal here is to make sure that the developers always have something to work on.

It often takes just minutes, and should never take longer than a few hours, for one person or team activity to break a story into tasks. As a result, it is relatively easy to ensure that there will always be ready tasks available to work on. Everything is steered by the volume of planned tasks in the task buffer. We recommend you start with a buffer size of 2 for this. So if there are just two tasks left, then one of the developers takes the next story from the product backlog and breaks it into tasks. If this buffer size of 2 proves too low—and you find your Ultimate Scrum projects sometimes empty the buffer before you can break the next story into tasks—you can simply increase the buffer size to 3 to prevent further "buffer holes" from occurring.

If buffer holes persist, then keep increasing the buffer size by one, until no buffer holes occur any more. If your buffer rises to the point at which you have more than one task in the buffer for every two developers, the problem most likely lies in how long it takes you to break stories into tasks. In practice, we can often achieve buffer sizes lower than 2, because it's usually easy to identify the first task of a story. So, even if the buffer is set to 0, pulling the next story and breaking out the first task can be done in minutes or even seconds.

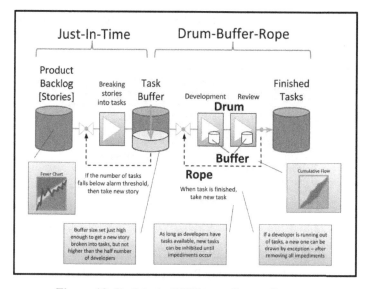

Figure 10: End-to-end Ultimate Scrum Process

To monitor the story burn down, we recommend updating the product burndown chart after each story is finished (as opposed to after each sprint). In addition, it is important to monitor the rate of project progress against the rate of the project's "scope buffer" used, as depicted in Figure 11. We will introduce how to monitor buffer consumption in the next chapter, but for now, it may be useful to know that it is a simple and effective way to manage project reliability, and will also be critically important for optimizing portfolio reliability—whether your portfolio is comprised only of Agile projects, or is a mix of IT project execution methodologies.

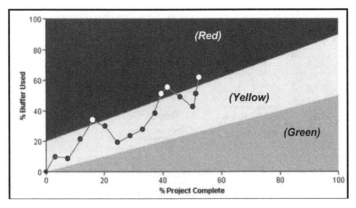

Figure 11: Monitoring Project Progress Against Buffer Consumption

In summary, Ultimate Scrum brings a number of compelling attributes when delivering Agile-based software-development projects. These attributes include:

- Continuous, single-piece flow in a pull system
- The fewest possible open tasks
- The shortest possible flow time and lead time

The result is maximum throughput of task completions, which speeds software-development projects and boosts project throughput. In our experience, adopting Ultimate Scrum will result in an additional 20-percent productivity improvement at the project level, even when taking into account that we've already eliminated multi-tasking and sprint-level commitments (and sprints, for that matter). Assuming that at least half of the typical project portfolio is comprised of software-development projects, this translates into an additional 10-percent throughput improvement across the portfolio. Figure 12 shows how Ultimate Scrum can further improve portfolio throughput for our hypothetical project portfolio.

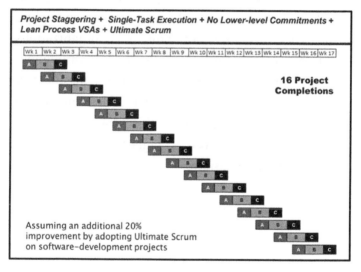

Figure 12: Throughput Benefits of Ultimate Scrum

Summary

We have presented five techniques for maximizing IT project portfolio throughput—Project Staggering, Single-task Execution, Elimination of Lower-level Commitments, Lean Process VSAs, and Ultimate Scrum. These techniques have origins in proven methods from Critical Chain, Lean, and Agile, though we have enhanced them with a few interesting innovations, and brought them together in a way that can potentially help you *quintuple* project throughput. We admit that we have yet to see more than a tripling in the real world, but we think most organizations would be pretty thrilled with a 3X throughput improvement. We should add that these "3X organizations" have yet to master all techniques in combination, as presented in this chapter. We are convinced that even higher breakthrough improvements are possible.

Chapter 4: How to Optimize Portfolio Reliability

The PMI survey cited in Chapter 1 reports that even organizations' highest-priority projects fail to deliver on their original goals and business intent 44 percent of the time; we can only presume that failure rate for the lower-priority projects is considerably higher than that. This failure rate is consistent with our experience—the typical project portfolio we see fails to deliver completed projects within plan about 60 percent of the time.

Given that projects are a risky business, achieving 100-percent reliability is likely to be unaffordable in both cost and schedule terms, no matter how good our portfolio reliability techniques may be. That said, however, some project portfolios carry more risk than others, and some organizations are more risk-averse than others. As a result, the optimal level of portfolio reliability will vary.

Because of this inherent variability, our aim is not to help you hit a specific reliability target, but rather to prescribe specific reliability-enhancing techniques that let you engineer the optimal reliability outcome for your IT project portfolio. We encourage you to aim high—for most portfolios, the optimal reliability target should be in the 90-95 percent range (or more than double the typical rate of about 40 percent).

Buffering

Most of us learned early in our PM training that the most fundamental building block of project-level reliability is buffering. In traditional project management, buffering has often been introduced as the "triple constraint rule," which holds that we must have some flexibility in schedule, budget, and/or scope in order to deliver with any hope of reliability. If all three are fixed, then the project is likely doomed to failure, and even the most naïve PM would be a fool to take on such a project.

Traditionally, **schedule buffers** have been the buffers of choice, as significant emphasis has been placed on defining scope and keeping it stable. In contrast, Agile defaults to **scope buffers**, under the premise that it's better to get started early in the scope-definition and refinement process, and use rapid iterations to tighten up scope as you go. Agile's reliance on scope buffers is also predicated on the assumption that, once the "must-have" components of scope are delivered, there will be a healthy backlog of "nice-to-have" features identified for development. These "nice-to-haves" are features that the customer will be happy to pay for, but which can also be sacrificed if the "must-haves" consume more time and effort than expected.[11]

In some circumstances, **budget buffers** will be preferable to schedule buffers. For example, one of the authors has a university as a client, and the majority of its IT projects must deliver a specific scope within an aggressive schedule (before the start of an upcoming semester), leaving little or no schedule buffer or scope buffer. As a result, budget buffers tend to predominate as the most feasible buffer type for them.

So, the concept of buffers isn't new, and our PMs are smart to pursue ample buffer for their projects, whether those buffers take the form of schedule, scope, or budget buffers, or some mix thereof. We also learned in Chapter 3 the value of aggregating risk by elevating buffers to the project level whenever possible. We must now address how project-level buffers can be used to improve portfolio reliability.

---

[11] Note that some Agile practitioners have begun to prefer schedule buffers over scope buffers, especially when the product owner has indicated a preference for this. For example, some product owners will still consider the lower-priority features as "must-have's," and be disappointed if they are not delivered. Similarly, they may prefer to call the project done once all must-have's are delivered.

Balancing Buffers Across the Project Portfolio

Project-level buffers are portfolio reliability assets—if an organization values the reliability of project completions, then project-level buffers are critical to achieving portfolio reliability. The rationale is simple—there will always be some projects that are healthier than others, and balancing this health is a powerful way to help optimize portfolio reliability.

For example, let's say there are only two projects in our portfolio, and that both are set to initiate execution on a critical architecture task that's expected to take 15 days. As we look to launch these two similar tasks, we learn that only one of the two architects originally assigned to them is now available, and that we have no good options for lining up an emergency replacement soon enough to make a difference. How should the organization resolve this resource conflict?

If we share the lone available architect across both projects, then we will slow both projects down, possibly causing both to fail. If we favor one project over the other—even if designated as a higher-priority project—we will probably cause the lower-priority project to fail, resulting in a lackluster portfolio reliability of 50 percent.

That outcome may be the best we can manage in this circumstance, but what if we had the situation shown in Figure 13—ample buffer remaining on one project, and at least some buffer on the other? In that scenario,

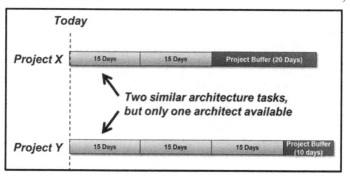

Figure 13: Balancing Project Buffers to Maximize Reliability

we have the option of assigning the architect to whichever project has less buffer, effectively balancing buffer levels across our two-project portfolio in order to maximize our chances of delivering *both* reliably.

Shown another way, the "fever chart" portfolio view in Figure 14 depicts Project Y getting the critical architect resource in order to avoid project failure, while Project X moves into the "red zone," but still with some buffer to protect against failure. While there is no guarantee that both projects will complete within plan, we have done what we can at the portfolio level to maximize the probability that both projects will land reliably. If the situation on either project worsens further, then we may need to prioritize which project should receive more protection so that at least one of them completes within plan.

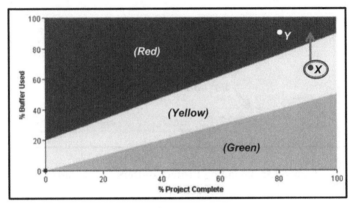

Figure 14: "Fever Chart" View of Balancing Buffers to Maximize Reliability

Of course, it is much more often the case that our project portfolios have more than just two projects, offering portfolio managers a wider variety of options for balancing buffers and optimizing portfolio reliability. An example of a typical 20-project portfolio is shown in Figure 15. As we can see, most projects are actually in the "yellow" zone, with just a handful in either red or green. While Projects X and Y are in a somewhat precarious situation, we have options for balancing buffers in an attempt to have both finish within plan. In the same breath, responsible portfolio managers will always strongly prefer to have

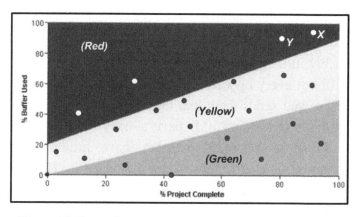

Figure 15: Fever Chart View of a Typical Project Portfolio Using BPI

individual projects explore all available internal options to bring themselves back to health, before healthier projects are asked to donate any of their hard-earned buffer as a "bail-out."

This fever-chart portfolio view plotting each project's percent complete vs. percent buffer used is called the "buffer protection index," or BPI, and comes from Critical Chain Project Management (CCPM). Most senior executives we work with usually end up relying on this BPI-based fever chart for their only portfolio dashboard view, as it gives them the ability to see a summary status of the entire portfolio, while focusing their attention only on those projects that need it.

This fever chart is also a favorite of high-performing PMs, because they tend to keep their projects very visibly in the green zone by conserving and protecting buffer at every opportunity. And when Murphy's Law strikes and sends them into the red zone occasionally, the high-performing PMs have already helped out so many of their peers, that they have little trouble garnering in-kind support when they need it. The end result is a strong unity of purpose among senior executives, PMs, and project-team members, as all are aligned under the common goal of bringing to completion as many projects as possible.

Reliability Benefits of Focused, Single-Task Execution

While we have already covered single-tasking as a technique for improving portfolio throughput in Chapter 3, it has the attractive "side benefit" of helping improve project-level reliability considerably. To illustrate how much more reliable single-tasking is, consider the results of a common simulation that we've run with dozens of groups. We'll ask the group to complete three simple "projects," such as listing the alphabet, a repeating pattern of numbers, and a repeating pattern of shapes. In Round 1, we'll ask everyone to task-switch constantly from one project to another. Then in Round 2, we'll ask everyone to single task, completing the entire alphabet first, then the number pattern, and finally the shape pattern.

As is evident from the results shown in Figure 16, not only is single-tasking roughly 40 percent faster on average, but the performance is also significantly more predictable, and therefore more reliable. It is also interesting to note that the worst single-tasking performers are about as good as the best task-switching performers. The results of this simulation suggest that we might reasonably convert even some of our below-average performers into heroes, simply by promoting single-task execution as the desired cultural norm.

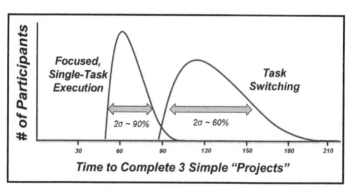

Figure 16: Reliability Benefits of Single-Task Execution

Reliability Benefits of Eliminating Task-level Commitments

Just as single-tasking offers compelling reliability advantages, so does the elimination of task-level commitments. As you'll recall from Chapter 3, this technique helped us achieve impressive throughput improvements by aggregating risk at the project level, encouraging aggressive performance without the need to self-insure against the risk of failing to meet a lower-level commitment.

Another simulation that we've run many times illustrates how eliminating lower-level commitments improves project-level reliability. To simulate the "pure chance" risk of failure that is part of task execution, we ask participants to roll a six-sided die until they get a "6." In Round 1, they roll on their own, and in Round 2, they roll in groups of three, effectively aggregating the risk of not rolling a 6.

While the "pure chance" aspect of this simulation may overstate the power of aggregating risk on projects, we have seen many examples of similarly unreliable performance, and we suspect that you have as well. For instance, we know that, on average, a single individual rolling a six-sided die will roll a "6" once for every six attempts. But the risk that it might sometimes take 20 rolls or more for that individual to actually deliver a "6" is frighteningly similar to what happens on some project tasks—the "tail" skews the distribution far to the right, to three or four times the expected average, severely degrading project reliability. But by aggregating this risk only modestly, we see how dramatic the reliability improvement can be.

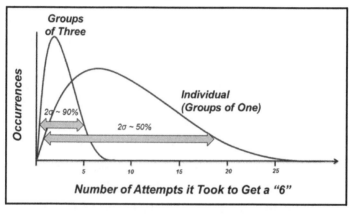

Figure 17: Reliability Benefits of Aggregating Risk

There is another way in which eliminating lower-level commitments helps improve reliability significantly. Recall the following graphic from Chapter 3, comparing task-level buffering with project-level buffering.

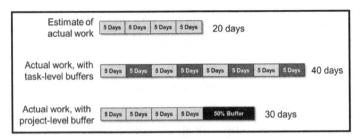

**Figure 18: Reliability Benefits of Project-level vs.
Task-level Buffering**

Under the task-level buffering approach, I can be on track all the way through the project, but then if things go awry on the final task, I only have that task's five-day buffer to protect the entire project from failing to complete within plan. Contrast this task-level approach with the project-level buffering approach, in which I am likely to have more than five days of buffer available when I reach the final task, because it's relatively rare that the first three tasks would go so badly that they consume 25 days out of my 30-day buffer. This aspect of risk aggregation is a powerful driver of improved project reliability.

Reliability Benefits of Software-enabling Lean Processes

In Chapter 3, we discussed how Lean Process VSAs can help drive up portfolio throughput by shrinking the process footprint of software-development projects. Shrinking the process footprint results in important reliability benefits as well. Specifically, business processes that have been "leaned out" are tighter and simpler, and can therefore be software-enabled with far less technical complexity. With less technical complexity, we get more predictable execution. While the impact of leaned-out processes will vary from project to project, we have seen examples in which most of the project-level reliability improvement is attributed to having much leaner business processes to software-enable.

Summary

We have presented five techniques for optimizing the reliability of IT project portfolios—Buffering, Buffer Balancing, Single-tasking, Elimination of Lower-level Commitments, and Software-enabling Lean Processes. Only the first two are "new" techniques, given that the other three were introduced in Chapter 3. And of those two, Buffering is a foundational PM technique that should be familiar to anyone with a PM background (though some detailed aspects of buffer sizing and managing multiple buffer types can get a bit complex). Buffer Balancing using the Buffer Protection Index (BPI) is a proven technique from CCPM, though we will be enhancing it a bit for "hybrid" portfolios in Chapter 6.

Chapter 5: Fight the Zealotry

This book's subtitle is "A Practical Approach for Applying the Best of Critical Chain, Agile, and Lean," and you've seen techniques from each of these, as well as from the Theory of Constraints, on which Critical Chain is based. We embrace this "best-tool-for-the-job" mindset as a practical matter, in our attempts to help pragmatic executives deliver the most impressive, real-world results possible.

Unfortunately, most of the advice we see being offered to CIOs and IT Project Portfolio Directors today seems rooted in zealotry. We regularly see Agile offered as the solution, before any questions are even asked about the problem. We've seen practitioners of differing approaches argue past each other, without even considering the possibility that they might have something to learn from one another. We've seen "one-size-fits-all" methods forced upon organizations, when it's clear to even a casual observer that some aspects simply must be tailored in order to help address those organizations' unique circumstances.

As your ally in the fight against such zealotry, we aim to add to your arsenal by shining a bright light on some of the more common examples of where fanatical adherence to a single approach can cause missed opportunities for improvement, or even degrade performance.

Examples of Misplaced Zealotry

Example #1: Agile's over-reliance on scope buffers. As discussed in Chapter 4, all PMs learn very early the importance of having flexibility, or buffers, in at least one part of the "triple constraint" (scope, schedule, and budget). So why limit ourselves to just one of those three? And what if a given project's needs call for a schedule buffer instead?

Agile presumes that customers or "product owners" never really know what they want with much specificity in the early phases of a software-development project, and that they are therefore best served by a scope buffer in order to have some needed flexibility on scope. Agile embeds this scope buffer into "the backlog" of software features, prioritized into "must-have" features, and one or more classes of "nice-to-have" features, often referred to as "desirements." Desirements = Scope Buffer.

But what if the scope is actually well defined, and likely to remain stable? What if the customer has no desirement features, or is unwilling to pay for them, preferring simply to finish the project once all required features are delivered? What if the customer is being driven by an aggressive schedule to deliver on a very tight scope?

In those scenarios, a scope buffer wouldn't really help, while a schedule buffer or budget buffer (or both) would be the better way to go. This doesn't mean that Agile has nothing to offer in those situations, but it does mean that Agile practitioners have to be more flexible and less dogmatic when it comes to proposing the right type of buffer. Some Agile practitioners understand this, and have begun to use a mix of both scope and schedule buffers.

Example #2: CCPM's over-reliance on schedule buffers. Just as Agile carries a built-in preference for scope buffers, CCPM does the same with schedule buffers, and presumes that due-date performance will always be really important, if not paramount. But what if it isn't? What if a given project's needs call for a scope buffer instead?

For many projects, incurring a schedule delay will result in a budget overrun, a scaled-back scope, or both, so CCPM practitioners argue that schedule problems are very often the "root cause" of budget and scope problems.

But this isn't always true—there are plenty of examples in which having an extended schedule *lowers* project cost, such as for "filler projects" that can be delivered primarily using existing resources during slack times.

Interestingly, it is relatively easy to show scope buffers as time-based, and usually straightforward to show budget buffers as time-based as well. We show how to do this in Chapter 6 when discussing how to manage a hybrid portfolio of both Agile and traditional projects. But CCPM's lack of flexibility in buffer type remains an issue, as it is still rare to find such flexibility in most major CCPM software offerings.[12]

Example #3: Agile's mistaken belief that sprints = focused execution. An Agile sprint is a short-duration

---

[12] The tide is turning, however, as we have influenced two CCPM software vendors to plan capabilities like this for future releases. Also, one of these vendors recently released functionality to integrate Ultimate Scrum at the task-execution level, and CCPM at the project and portfolio levels. While it is not the purpose of this book to recommend specific software tools, feel free to contact us if you'd like more information on these vendors.

"time box," usually spanning 1-4 weeks, into which scrum-team members organize their tasks. The primary purpose of a sprint is to encourage focused execution in the face of a near-term deadline. However, it turns out that many people are actually *less* productive under the stress of a near-term deadline, and deliver *lower-quality* work, especially if they are constantly under the pressure of near-term deadlines.

And when team members are more productive in a sprint, it's as a result of shutting out all distractions and performing in a focused, single-tasked manner, as laid out in Chapters 3 and 4. In fact, for every example we've seen in which Agile seems to improve productivity, we see focused, single-task execution predominate—especially using Ultimate Scrum. Similarly, for every example we've seen in which Agile seems to disappoint, we see a heavily task-switched culture that values responsiveness and "ability to multi-task" highly.

So if focused, single-task execution is the best way for all team members to maximize their productive work effort, then such focus should be what we explicitly encourage, whether we do it as part of a sprint or not. And if some members of the team don't respond well to the constant pressure of near-term deadlines, then maybe it's better to do away with sprints altogether. Finally, as we saw in Chapter 3's discussion of Ultimate Scrum, the "task batching" aspect of sprints is an impediment to maximizing the flow of productive work, so rather than forcing a somewhat arbitrary sprint deadline that may well disrupt work mid-stream, allowing some flexibility on when and how to package up finished work offers a higher-productivity option.

Example #4: Lean's over-emphasis on big deployments. Lean, whether paired with Six Sigma or not, offers a wide array of tools and techniques that are often used in conjunction with one another to maximize their process-improvement effectiveness. Lean also emphasizes the importance of executive commitment to achieving meaningful results, and the importance of having everyone trained to apply Lean philosophy and techniques wherever they can across the organization. Doing all of this together has worked for some organizations, but for far too many others, it presents itself as an impractical, "boil the ocean" approach.

It is possible to apply select few Lean techniques to specific target problem areas, reap the benefits, and repeat—as we have proposed with Lean Process VSAs in Chapters 3 and 4, and with Ultimate Scrum's single-piece flow in Chapter 3. While there are additional Lean concepts bundled in with our discussion, and some likelihood that additional Lean techniques might be needed to complement the few we've introduced in this book, we do our best to avoid throwing too many tools at too many problems, preferring instead to keep things focused on select few "best tools for the job."

Example #5: Agile's over-emphasis on the self-managed and self-organized team. Autonomy and empowerment can be wonderful motivators, as can being an effective member of a high-performing team. We take no issue with these aspects of a self-managed team, especially as applied to project-level challenges. The portfolio-level implications are another matter, however.

First, there is often the misplaced notion that the self-managed team is an island unto itself, and not a set of portfolio resources that can and should be allocated to where the portfolio needs them the most. This creates unnecessary stove-piping across the portfolio, rather than promoting portfolio-wide unity of purpose.

Second, there is often the overly fervent emphasis on the sanctity of maintaining an intact team, rebelling against any attempt to pull one scrum-team member off temporarily to go help out another project that may need that individual's skill set. We understand the benefits of having team members work together through challenges over time, build trust with one another, learn to complement each other better, enhance velocity, and learn from one another and grow. But let's get real here—allowing your software architect to help another team work through its architecture challenges for a couple weeks, during what would otherwise have been a relatively slow time for her, is a smart move, and won't be catastrophic for team performance.

Finally, this overemphasis on the self-managed team sometimes encourages petulant attitudes toward executive leadership. This attitude manifests itself in statements such as, "We don't need no stinkin' managers to oversee us!" or "Yeah, our project hit a couple snags, but getting beat up over it by a bunch of stuffed suits in a status meeting won't get it solved!"

We understand that senior executives don't always do the right thing, and that in general, they need to take on more of a "get behind and push" mentality, instead of the all too common approach of "clobbering" projects that are already suffering. But let's face facts—every employee is, first and foremost, an organizational resource. And thus, every employee should be encouraged to help wherever their impact can be maximized. Conversely, no employee should ever be devoted exclusively to addressing the insular concerns of the small team to which they happen to be assigned. This rule should be reinforced at every opportunity, with all staff.

Summary

Hopefully, this small handful of examples will help arm you with information you can use in your quest for a deliberate, practical, best-tool-for-the-job approach, and better enable you push your consultants and your teams to offer more than you could by blindly following any single approach.

Chapter 6: The Best of Both Worlds

The book *Critical Chain* was first published in 1997, with the *Agile Manifesto* following not long after in 2001. Yet despite over a decade of co-existence, we have seen only a handful of attempts to harness the advantages of both for a single project portfolio. And when the two communities do engage, the engagements tend to take on an oppositional tone.

We see three fundamental similarities between CCPM and Agile, however:

1) Both subscribe to the foundational PM principle of **buffering** to improve project reliability.
2) Both place emphasis on **focused execution** to improve flow and speed.
3) Both understand the importance of **aggregating risk** in order to improve speed and reliability.

We believe these three similarities present major opportunities to apply techniques from both Agile and CCPM in a harmonious way. We have already presented most of those techniques in Chapters 3 and 4. This chapter will show how to integrate both harmoniously, while also providing some advice on when to use which, so that your IT project portfolio can benefit from the best of both worlds.

Buffer Balancing: The Integration Touch Point

As described in Chapter 4, the most effective portfolio-level reliability technique we know of is Buffer Balancing, as it gives portfolio managers a single, straightforward view of each project's buffer status, along with options for having healthy projects lend a hand to less healthy ones when desirable. So if Agile, CCPM, and more traditional projects all use some type of project-level buffering, then all we need is an "apples-to-apples" view of each project's buffer status, graphed consistently in a fever chart based on the Buffer Protection Index (BPI).

As mentioned in Chapter 5, this approach is relatively straightforward for schedule and scope buffers, which are also the most common buffer types. While converting a budget buffer to either a scope or schedule buffer is a bit trickier, it is usually still feasible to do. For example, in Figure 19, we provide a time-based view of all three buffer types.

In the first example, we see a schedule buffer, which of course is already time-based. In the second example, we see an Agile project with four sprints—each of which has a known duration—but we've simply renamed Sprint 4 "Scope Buffer."[13] As long as we can reasonably estimate how much schedule is required to

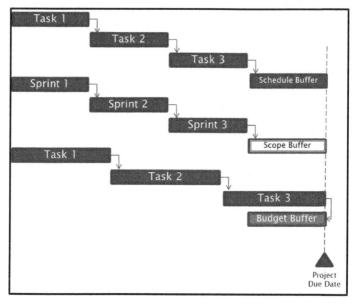

Figure 19: Showing All Three Buffer Types as Time-based

[13] While we encourage elimination of sprints in favor of Ultimate Scrum's continuous task flow, we use sprints here to simplify discussion of scope buffers. With no sprints, the Ultimate Scrum task flow would be harder to show in this simple Gantt-chart example, but the scope buffer would appear the same, taking the same amount of planned time.

deliver a given chunk of scope, showing our scope buffers as time-based is simple.

In the third example, we see a budget buffer depicted as time-based. There are a few challenges in doing this. First is the finish-to-finish dependency, which essentially just means that we need to finish all project tasks before our budget buffer is exhausted. Second is estimating how much schedule a given level of budget will buy us. On labor-intensive projects, this usually just requires a few simple calculations on how much schedule acceleration we can achieve by "crashing" the schedule with additional staff resources. On capital-intensive projects, we may have to perform a more detailed assessment of just how much schedule or scope some additional budget might buy us. This includes "buy vs. build" options, such as buying an expensive piece of commercial software in lieu of developing similar functionality internally.

Such challenges notwithstanding, we now have a straightforward approach for showing all buffers in an apples-to-apples, time-based manner—offering PMs a familiar Gantt-chart view of their buffers, and providing portfolio managers visibility into portfolio-wide buffer status, with options to balance them when advantageous to do so.

If a scope-buffered Agile project is healthy, and a schedule-buffered traditional project is hopelessly in the red zone, then a portfolio manager can reallocate resources from the Agile project to the traditional project. The only cost is sacrificing some of the Agile project's desirement features (scope buffer), while the benefit is a highly reliable project portfolio. Of course, the reverse is also true—a healthy schedule-buffered project can have some resources reallocated to a less healthy scope-buffered project, so that the probability of *both* projects completing within plan is maximized.

As depicted in the IT project portfolio in Figure 20, we can show the status of each project and its buffer, by buffer type. This way, the portfolio manager can know when using one type of buffer to help out a project

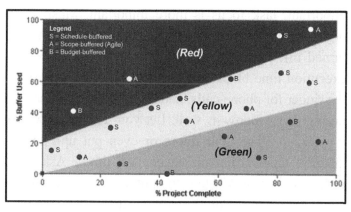

Figure 20: Portfolio View of BPI by Buffer Type

with a different type of buffer might require some additional consideration.

Focused Execution

As mentioned in previous chapters, focused, single-task execution can drive substantial improvements in speed and reliability, regardless of which project delivery approach we adopt. CCPM calls for this directly, and Agile's sprints were also designed with this in mind, giving us another area of strong alignment between the two approaches.

The key here is to do everything you can to de-value that which disrupts single-tasking, and establish a "new norm" that values focused execution above all else. Let your teams know that, while responsiveness is important, task focus is more important. Make it an organizational default to have Outlook pop-up notifiers turned off. Block off IM availability during focused-execution time blocks, and while you're at it, turn off the ringer for phone calls, and alerts for text messaging during that window as well. Let your teams know that it's OK to close their doors or even put up "do not disturb" tape during task-execution times. Ask your PMs and Scrum Masters to protect their teams from emails and calls from senior executives and clients, using out-of-office messages if necessary. Ask all team members to block off, say, six hours every day on their calendars for focused task work, leaving the rest of the time to respond to messages and address ad-hoc issues.

Oh, and if your scrum teams seem to thrive on the constant pressure of sprint deadlines and prefer that you keep them, then we suggest you conduct an experiment comparing speed and performance with, and without, sprints and sprint deadlines. We predict that they will find the performance improvements of no sprints and no deadlines very compelling. If your scrum teams are ready to explore the possible benefits of pursuing continuous flow while doing away with sprints altogether, then give it a go. If you get significant resistance on eliminating sprints altogether, then allow them to persist, but continue to emphasize continuous flow over sprint deadlines. Before long, the team will often realize that sprints and sprint deadlines are unnecessary.

Aggregated Risk

While both Agile and CCPM offer ways to aggregate risk, CCPM advocates elevating this risk to the project and portfolio levels whenever beneficial, and whenever acceptable to the customer. In contrast, Agile focuses its risk aggregation on the scrum team, ignoring the benefits of aggregating risk to the highest level feasible. There's no reason Agile projects can't also benefit by aggregating the risk beyond the scrum team, to the project level.

Similarly, there's no reason non-Agile projects can't benefit from the additional risk-aggregation benefits of a scrum-team approach. For example, a high-functioning, high-velocity scrum team will have developed significant areas of overlap in knowledge, skills, and situational awareness on the project, fostering a much more fluid ability to progress through tasks in the face of any unforeseen staff disruptions. As a result, such disruptions might well be handled seamlessly, avoiding the need to consume any project buffer in order to resolve them.

Summary

We have identified three fundamental similarities between Agile and CCPM: Buffering, Focused Execution, and Risk Aggregation. By representing all project buffers as time-based, we can balance them across the project portfolio when desirable, thus boosting portfolio reliability while maintaining flexibility in whichever project delivery method we choose. By establishing single-tasking as the norm, all approaches will see productivity jump. And by aggregating risk at the project level on all projects, and at the task level using scrum-team approaches when it makes sense, you will achieve improvements in both speed and reliability. Such improvements simply would not have been possible with just a single delivery method, but integrated together harmoniously, you can harness the best of both worlds.

Chapter 7: Putting It All Together

This book has presented nine techniques from six distinct origins, spanning the Theory of Constraints, Critical Chain, Agile, Lean, and a couple of innovative "add-on" approaches developed by the authors. No technique is overly complicated, and all are proven, yet this book is the first to bring them together harmoniously into a single, integrated PPM framework designed to pick the highest-impact projects, and to deliver as many of them as possible, as reliably as possible.

Technique	Origin(s)	Primary Purpose
Project Selection Using Effective ROI	Theory of Constraints	• Select high-impact projects
Project Staggering	Critical Chain Project Management (CCPM)	• Boost Portfolio Throughput • Expose Resource Bottlenecks
Single-Tasking	CCPM, Agile, Others	• Speed Project Execution • Improve Project Reliability
Eliminating Task-Level Commitments	CCPM	• Speed Project Execution • Improve Project Reliability
Process VSA	Lean	• Tighten Scope • Reduce Complexity
Buffering Techniques	CCPM, Agile, Others	• Improve Project Reliability
Buffer Balancing	CCPM	• Improve Portfolio Reliability
How to Manage a Hybrid Agile / Traditional IT Project Portfolio	FORTEZZA CONSULTING	• "Best Tool for the Job" Flexibility • Helps Avoid Zealotry
Ultimate Scrum	▷▷▷ SPEED 4 projects	• Speed Project Execution

Figure 21: The Nine Techniques, Their Origins, and Primary Purpose

While the three of us agree on the breakthrough potential of combining these techniques as described in this book, we each have emphasized some over others in practice. This is largely attributable to our diverse backgrounds and focus areas—Wolfram has focused more on large-scale software development portfolios in the European private sector; Mike on a mix of software development, COTS implementation, and IT infrastructure portfolios in the U.S. public and private sectors; and Hilbert on a wide variety of IT, construction, manufacturing, and other project portfolios all over the world. As a result, Hilbert might typically focus on seven of the nine techniques, while Wolfram normally bundles a slightly different mix into a combination of "Reliable Scrum" (based on CCPM) and Ultimate Scrum, and Mike looks to apply the total technique set under the name "ACCLAIM™ PPM" (Advanced Critical Chain, Lean, and Agile Integration Methods). So while there is some flexibility to apply slightly different subsets of the nine techniques, some aspects are non-negotiable—here they are:

1) Project selection is best governed by Effective ROI.

2) At the task level, Single Tasking is the best way to maximize improvements in speed and

reliability, followed by the Elimination of Commitments.

3) At the project level, Project Staggering is the best way to boost the throughput of project completions, while monitoring time-based buffers is the best way to boost reliability.

4) At the portfolio level, Buffer Balancing using the Buffer Protection Index (BPI) is the best way to optimize reliability.

These non-negotiable components are all based on the Theory of Constraints and CCPM (which is itself a TOC application). This makes sense, as TOC focuses on the underlying drivers of system-wide performance optimization. But there are multiple concepts from Lean and Agile built into these techniques as well, with compelling performance-enhancing benefits.

Let's organize all techniques visually according to Task Level, Project Level, and Portfolio Level, starting with the Task Level. Figure 22 shows all four task-level techniques together: Single Tasking, No Task-level Commitments, Lean Process VSAs, and Ultimate Scrum.

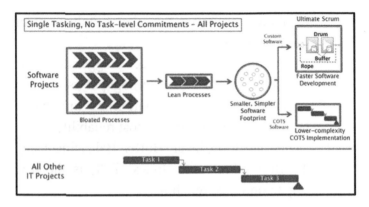

Figure 22: Task-level View

Figure 23 shows the three project-level techniques together: Project Staggering, Project Buffering, and Showing All Buffers as Time-Based.[14]

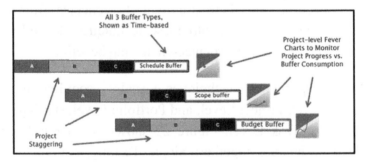

Figure 23: Project-level View

[14] Note that Project Staggering is technically a portfolio-level technique; we show it at the project level to draw attention to the individual projects and their differing buffer types, while also conveying the staggering relationships among the individual projects.

Figure 24 shows the two Portfolio-level techniques: Project Selection using Effective ROI, and Buffer Balancing according to the Buffer Protection Index (BPI).

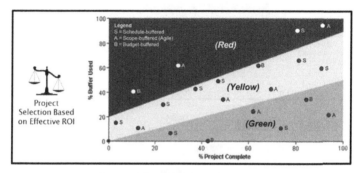

Figure 24: Portfolio-level View

And finally, here is the combined picture for all nine techniques, integrated together:

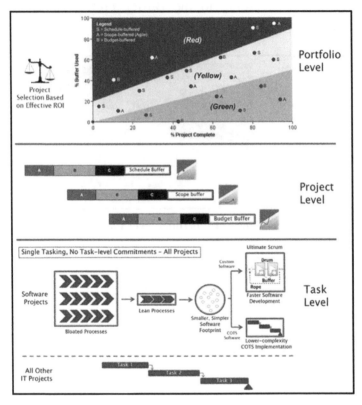

Figure 25: View of All Levels Combined

The touch points connecting all three levels are simple. Project selection is a portfolio-level responsibility that governs the introduction of new projects, which are visible at the portfolio level and executed in a staggered manner at the project level. Staggering projects effectively requires identification of task-level dependencies, resource-loading and resource-leveling. For software-development activities, we can decompose tasks down to a very granular level, and organize task execution using Drum-Buffer-Rope. As tasks progress at the task level, progress and buffer consumption are monitored at the project level, while the portfolio view provides a snapshot status for all projects.

Chapter 8: Overcoming Obstacles

We suspect that most readers have risen to executive ranks by being effective change agents, and that they therefore understand the challenges inherent in pursuing dramatic performance improvements. With this in mind, we thought it would be helpful to identify the primary obstacles you're likely to face as you attempt to introduce the techniques laid out in this book, as well as strategies for overcoming these obstacles.

Obstacle #1: Convincing stakeholders that staggering their project for a late start will actually result in an earlier finish.

The strategy for overcoming this obstacle has three parts:

1) Walk stakeholders through the staggering example provided in Chapter 3, so that they can see the concept, ask questions, and challenge it if they so choose.[15]

---

[15] For a free download that simulates how staggering can help improve portfolio performance, go to http://speed4projects.net/fileadmin/downloads/BeadsGame.exe.

2) Let them know that you understand any
   skepticism they may have—after all, given the
   lackluster track record of most IT projects, they
   are reasonable to question whether starting a
   project months late might actually result in an
   earlier finish.

3) Implement staggering in just one business unit
   or portfolio, ideally all for the same stakehold-
   er, to demonstrate its effectiveness before
   rolling out across the organization (see Chapter
   9 for more on this).

Obstacle #2: Adopting single-tasking as the norm

There are dozens of little things that can and should be
done, many of which we have offered up in Chapter 6,
but there are two overarching strategies that will
significantly accelerate adoption:

1) Communicate that the organization now values
   focusing on priorities more than on being
   responsive. Let everyone know that there will
   be times in which it will be tempting to show
   responsiveness—even times when supervisors
   will demand responsiveness—and that these
   must all be challenged.

2) For all of the challenged examples of responsiveness called out in #1, identify those that really do still require a level of responsiveness, and develop a solution for each that continues to protect single-tasking.

For example, let's say your best customer enjoys working closely with one of your senior developers, and regularly comments favorably on how responsive that developer is. Explain to that customer that this developer will continue to be responsive, but only between 3-5pm, and that if the issue is too urgent to wait until then, they must contact the PM or Scrum Master during protected focus hours.

When coming up with solutions like this, a good model to keep in mind is a well-run school. Teachers are expected to focus on teaching one lesson at a time, through to completion, during scheduled class periods. If a concerned parent calls demanding responsiveness on an issue during scheduled class periods, the school makes sure the call is handled immediately, but explains that the teacher is teaching at the moment, and that the issue will be addressed during dedicated time after class periods. Only under the most urgent scenarios would the teacher's class be disturbed.

Obstacle #3: Convincing PMs and Scrum Masters to abandon task-level deadlines

Meeting commitments, holding people accountable, setting clear expectations—these are but a few of the mantras we've all heard over and over from senior leaders and management experts. And we agree that all are pretty important. We don't agree, however, that these mantras should manifest as task-level deadlines—the cost in terms of speed and reliability is simply too high.

A good model here is a relay race. All runners are motivated to perform as well as they can for their individual leg of the race, even though they may have no chance at a medal, fame, or sponsorship money. They enjoy doing this, even though it requires hard work and often a fair amount of pain. They simply want to perform well, and are proud to do their part to help the team. It also helps that there are usually people watching—no one wants to embarrass themselves in front of others by not giving their best effort.

No runners are asked to commit to a specific time or speed—and if you did ask them, they would likely look at you like you're nuts, because all athletes know that performance will vary from one race to the next.

If we can set up our task-execution environments to more closely resemble a relay race, the behaviors will follow—as will the speed and reliability benefits.

Obstacle #4: Convincing process owners and participants to let go of their non-value-added steps.

There are three components to doing this right:

1) Training process owners and participants on the importance of eliminating such bloat, with examples of the benefits realized when others have done it, as well as examples of how to overcome resistance that may exist among other process participants.

2) Establishing an executive sponsor or "champion" to emphasize how important it is to eliminate non-value-added steps, and invoking their authority to push past resistance. If you are the CIO or IT PMO Director, you may be the best choice for the champion role, or there

may be a COO or similar role that carries the right level of authority to make this work.

3) Communicating the benefits—both in the speed and reliability of the improved process slated for software enablement, and in the speed and reliability of the software-development project to support it. Once people see the big impact they can have, they tend to get onboard quickly.

Obstacle #5: Convincing scrum-team members to abandon sprints in favor of Ultimate Scrum's continuous flow

If your scrum teams strongly resist abandoning sprints, it's usually because of how sprints have protected them from disruptions—so if you can show them another way to offer this same protection, they may be more receptive. For example, if the organization has demonstrated that it wants single-tasking to become the norm, and wants more mature buffer-management discipline using project-level fever charts like the one shown in Figure 11 on page 66, then scrum-team members may get all the reassurance they need.

Another approach that has proved effective is simply to keep the sprints while introducing the continuous flow approach of Ultimate Scrum—then over time, as the team begins to see that sprints aren't really necessary, the sprints simply wither away.

Obstacle #6: Convincing executive stakeholders to avoid cutting buffers

When executive stakeholders first see how large a project-level schedule buffer appears, their natural inclination is to cut it down a bit, and show an earlier finish. What they may not realize is that all task-level buffers have already been removed, and that the project-level buffer represents all the protection there is. As a result, executive stakeholders must be trained to protect buffers, not cut them.

Interestingly, Agile's scope buffering can be a useful deterrent in this regard. Because executive stakeholders see actual desirement features in the scope buffer, they see potential value that they may be more hesitant to cut. A schedule buffer, on the other hand, might just appear as unnecessary "dead time" that can be cut with no impact.[16]

Obstacle #7: Convincing PMs and Scrum Masters to lend their project resources to at-risk projects.

This is usually a lot easier than it might seem initially. In a traditional PM environment, getting PMs and scrum masters to share project resources is often exceedingly difficult, as PMs tend to see one another more as competitors than as peers. They correctly perceive their path to success through the success of their particular project. Therefore, anything that adds risk to their project—such as lending a key resource to a peer—is avoided like a disease.

Once the portfolio buffer balancing described in this book is in play, however, the entire success model changes fundamentally. We send the clear message that the organization values portfolio throughput and reliability over the success or failure of one individual project. We also make clear that conserving and

---

[16] Note that this is a double-edged sword, however, as some executives become very disappointed when they learn that their scope-buffered projects must sacrifice some desirement features, whereas sacrificing some schedule doesn't risk getting hopes up on features that may not be delivered.

protecting buffer is both a project-level and portfolio-level priority, and that the portfolio-wide buffers are there to protect everyone from the risk of going too far into the red zone.

This approach tends to work so well, so quickly, that it's usually just a few weeks or months until PMs begin to offer help to their peers *without prompting*, leaving portfolio managers free to focus on those projects that really need their attention.

The only possible challenge is, for Agile projects, the belief that the scrum team must remain intact. This notion still predominates, so the idea of having scrum teams lend out team members to other teams may be perceived as disrupting the team dynamic that has been so carefully cultivated among those specific team members. However, because scrum-team members already embrace a value system that places shared goals over individual goals, elevating that value system to the entire portfolio is usually received well in concept. The details will need to be negotiated between portfolio level and project level, assessing what the true impact to the affected scrum team might be, weighed against the hoped-for benefit to the project that needs the help. The key, of course, is maintaining unity of purpose across all levels, and fostering the trust required for such changes to be adopted and given a fair chance of success.

Obstacle #8: Project portfolios comprised mostly of fixed-price contracts.

If your project portfolio contracts out a significant number of its projects, and those contracts are structured as fixed price, then this will hinder your ability to balance buffers across projects. Balancing buffers requires the flexibility to reallocate resources from healthier projects to at-risk ones, and fixed-price contracts are not set up to provide this flexibility—especially if the "lender" and "borrower" of reallocated resources are different companies.

Solution options and workarounds do exist, but let's start by pointing out that a significant number of contracted projects is usually not as big a problem for portfolio reliability as it might at first seem. While fixed-price contracts present some impediments to buffer balancing (and are therefore usually not optimal for portfolio reliability), the reliability benefits to be obtained through the other techniques presented in this book are often more than enough to offset those impediments.

In any case, some buffer balancing can still be accomplished with portfolios that rely heavily on fixed-price contracts—here are some examples:

1) If one contractor has multiple projects in your portfolio, they may already do some form of buffer balancing across these projects. If they don't, encourage them to do so, and to share the results with you.

2) Use contract modifications as a surrogate for buffer balancing. This will never be as flexible or as effective as simply reassigning resources from one project to another; but issuing contract modifications to adjust a project's schedule, scope, or budget—while providing financial rewards to high-performing contracts that might otherwise perceive any reduction as punishment—can improve portfolio reliability.

3) Add time-and-materials options to fixed-price contracts, allowing both flexibility and the ability to reward your higher-performing contractors with additional work.

4) Use buffer balancing on your internal staff resources, even if they only form a fraction of

total portfolio resources. Benefits may be a mere fraction of what they would be for the whole portfolio, but this "lead by example" approach can be a start, and send a strong message to your contractors on how you'd like to improve portfolio reliability.

On a final note, keep in mind that getting rid of fixed-price contracts may not be as hard as you think. One of the authors (Hilbert) has served clients with sizable portfolios of construction projects, which are nearly always contracted out as fixed price. In some cases, those clients have realized the unnecessary portfolio risk these fixed-price contracts introduce, and have found creative ways to restructure them as time-and-materials, rewarding the high performers with more work in a win-win scenario.

Chapter 9: How to Get Started

We have consulted on "big bang" approaches and have helped them succeed, especially if there is a strong sense of urgency to improve project portfolio performance as much as possible, as soon as possible. While this approach carries some risk and a lot of visibility, the benefits will be more than worth it—and equally visible. If you're not sure you're ready for such an enterprise approach, and would strongly prefer some kind of pilot, we advise a large-scale one, such as for an entire business unit's IT project portfolio. The reason is that small pilots typically yield small results, while introducing conflicting value systems across the organization.

For example, how effective would it be to have single-task focus for just some members of your team? There are important human processes of learning new techniques, adopting new value systems, overcoming unforeseen cultural hurdles, and advancing up the maturity curve—and these are much easier when done with maximum participation and organizational alignment.

We wish that having a nice little pilot off to the side would demonstrate great benefits with minimal risk, as is often the case with many software pilots. But the nature of pursuing breakthrough performance improvement across the project portfolio is different, and we have learned this the hard way. We have tried piloting these techniques many times, in many industries all over the world, and have simply found that small pilots tend to lose more momentum than they build.

Recommended Sequence of Technique Adoption

While we do recommend organization-wide rollouts, we do not advise attempting to adopt all techniques all at once. Here is the logical progression that we recommend:

1) **Project Staggering**: A great way to begin focusing attention on organizational capacity for projects, to expose resource bottlenecks, and to get some near-term portfolio throughput benefits. Staggering also helps pave the way for single-task execution, as it provides a portfolio-level example of the benefits of completing things, and avoiding taking on more than can be handled effectively.

2) **Project Buffering**: You are likely doing some type of project buffering already, but in our experience, most organizations can get a lot of benefit by focusing on how to use the three buffer types with greater discipline and maturity. Project buffering is also a great way to begin focusing on the importance of project reliability, so just having discussions on how much buffer is appropriate, and what type is appropriate, can yield real benefits. You will also begin to gain experience with the fever chart for monitoring buffer consumption as your projects progress

3) **Portfolio Buffer Balancing**: Once you have projects staggered and buffered, and have experience monitoring buffer consumption with the fever chart, it will be a straightforward next step to try balancing buffers across the portfolio. The key here is restraint—just because you *can* rebalance buffers, doesn't always mean that you should. It's always better to try and work through project-level solutions to regaining buffer first, than to move resources all over the portfolio every time something goes wrong.

4) **Project Selection Using Effective ROI**: Once you have projects staggered and buffered, and some experience managing buffers across the portfolio, you will then have a clearer sense of how to apply the Effective ROI thinking, and can also begin to enjoy the benefits of being able to put more projects into the queue.

5) **Eliminating Task-level Commitments**: Most practitioners advise doing this step in concert with Project Buffering, as it is very beneficial to expose hidden task-level buffers while trying to establish and protect a generous project-level buffer. We like that approach as well, and think that most portfolios may want this technique implemented earlier anyway, given that most projects simply can't afford to carry the hidden buffers on top of the project-level buffers. We only list it as #5 in the event that you find it easier to adopt one technique at a time, and prefer to lock in the benefits of some of the other techniques first. Also, this technique requires some trust-building—which can take a little time. Furthermore, it sometimes meets with resistance, and so it tends to be less of a "quick win" technique to start with.

6) **Single-tasking**: This is where you will begin to achieve breakthrough levels of performance improvement, but it is also the technique that may require the biggest shift in organizational culture. It can take time to reorient value systems away from responsiveness and ability to juggle many things at once, toward the speedy and reliable completion of open tasks.

7) **Ultimate Scrum**: For software-development projects, this technique builds on #5 and #6 very effectively, driving speed and flow of task execution up another 20-30 percent.

8) **Showing all Buffers as Time-Based**: This technique can be done as early as #4, and if your portfolio is a hybridized mix of Agile and traditional projects, you may want to start this as soon as possible, so that you can harmonize your portfolio under a single PPM framework.

9) **Lean Process VSAs**: This can be a very high-powered technique, and we save it for last only because we think it's more important to get good at the other techniques first. Also, while Process VSAs are applicable to both custom software-development and COTS implementa-

tion projects, they are most powerful on projects that are very process-heavy. Note that you could apply this technique at any point in the sequence—even as the first one—and get great benefit from it.

Characteristics of an Ideal Large-scale Pilot

If you must pilot, and are looking to structure a large-scale one that is set up for success, here are our suggestions for you. The ideal large-scale pilot:

1) Has the unwavering support of the entire executive team.
2) Has at least ten projects in the initiation and planning stages.
3) Already shares a common resource pool of at least 100 staff.
4) Already shares a common set of project stakeholders.
5) Has project stakeholders and staff who are eager to see improvements, and willing to support improvement efforts.
6) Has a competent consultant to coach and mentor along the way.

The reasons why it's ideal to have total executive support should be obvious, but you might ask, "Can it work with just a few executive champions?" Yes, it can, especially if the executive champions carry enough clout to convince others of the importance of getting on board. In those cases, a handful of champions can get us closer to the ideal scenario of total executive support.

As for the optimum number of projects, going below ten runs the risk of suboptimal results for the pilot. You'll still see project-level benefits in those cases, but portfolio-level benefits will not be as apparent. While it is ideal for all projects to be in the initiation and planning stages, it's okay if a couple of them are already kicked off.

As for having a common resource pool of at least 100 staff, it's easier if the necessary resources are already aligned. If, however, you have more than one resource pool that you'd like to apply to your pilot, you will want to merge them, even if just temporarily for the duration of the pilot. This is particularly important for buffer balancing, as you'll want the flexibility to reassign resources.

Similarly, the more stakeholders you have in common across the large-scale pilot, the easier it will be to train them on the "new rules," and the easier it will be to manage them. Likewise, having supportive stakeholders and staff will ease adoption issues, especially through the early mistakes that are common. We are not suggesting that you should turn away all of the skeptics—a little healthy skepticism and critical thinking can be enormously beneficial, as long as attitudes in general aren't negative.

And of course, having a qualified consultant to advise, coach, and mentor you and your teams through the adoption and maturation process can help a lot. In addition to selecting one with the right technical knowledge and experience, we strongly suggest bringing on a consultant schooled in multiple improvement philosophies and approaches.

There are lots of reasons for taking such an agnostic approach, but the most important is that IT organizations today typically have adherents to a diverse set of models and techniques, and thus will have differing opinions on when to use which. The consultant must be well-versed enough to address all major questions and challenges from the variety of adherents, without just steam-rolling over the ones who may not subscribe to their preferred approach.

That should be enough to get you started. For additional information and tools, check out www.FortezzaConsulting.com and www.Reliable-Scrum.info.

Feel free to drop us a line and ask any questions you may have, share challenges, and tell us about your progress. We also welcome any feedback on how we might strengthen our approach.

Appendix: When to Use Agile, and When Not to

Agile can be a highly effective way to drive up the productivity of software-development teams—especially when modified using Ultimate Scrum and associated techniques in this book, such as single-tasking and elimination of task-level commitments. We also agree that many aspects of Agile can be applied successfully beyond just software-development projects. For example, Agile's "retrospective" is a beneficial practice that has existed long before Agile, and has often been called a "lessons learned session," similar to what the U.S. military calls an "after-action review," or AAR.

As a result, when we offer advice on when *not* to use Agile, we're not saying that all Agile techniques must be eliminated from consideration. Rather, we're saying that the combined set of what we consider Agile's core elements—including the product backlog, the frequent delivery of incremental software capabilities, and frequent customer interaction to refine scope—can be highly effective in some IT project scenarios, and suboptimal or ineffective in others.[17]

Similarly, when we offer advice on when Agile makes sense, we're not saying that Agile is the only effective way to perform incremental software delivery, or to promote customer transparency and intimacy. We are saying that it can be a great approach, worth serious consideration—especially if using Ultimate Scrum.

Finally, we understand that there may well be a host of additional considerations when deciding which execution methodology is best for a given project. Chief among these could be how well your current staff know Agile, and how experienced they are at applying it. As such, this guide is intended to highlight key considerations that are often overlooked, as opposed to serving as a comprehensive manual for all possible considerations.

---

[17] Note that we deliberately omit sprints from this list. While we acknowledge that sprints are regarded as a core element of Agile as commonly practiced, we recommend that sprints be eliminated in favor of Ultimate Scrum's continuous flow approach, as described in Chapter 3.

The decision tree in Figure 26 lays out our logic for when Agile should be seriously considered, and when it should be removed from consideration. As an additional bonus, we have incorporated logic for when to use Lean Process VSAs in our decision tree as well,

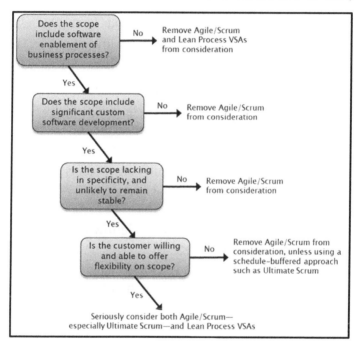

Figure 26: Decision Tree for When to Use Agile and Lean Process VSAs

given that they tend to be most impactful on software projects (both custom-developed and commercial off-the-shelf [COTS] software).

As shown in the figure, we believe only four questions need be asked—here is our rationale for each:

1) Does the scope include software-enablement of business processes?

We ask this because both Agile and Lean Process VSAs offer significant benefits to software projects. As discussed in Chapter 3, Lean Process VSAs can help shrink the process footprint of both custom-developed and COTS software, significantly tightening scope to drive dramatic speed improvements. Neither Agile nor Process VSAs as we've proposed using them in this book will be very helpful on projects that are not software-enabling a business process.

2) Does the scope include significant custom software development?

We ask this because Agile is far more applicable for custom software development than it is for COTS implementations, while Lean Process VSAs can be very effective for both.

3) Is the scope lacking in specificity, and unlikely to remain stable?

We ask this because Agile is far more applicable for scenarios in which scope requires significant refinement, and is likely to change frequently through the course of the project. Consider, for example, a construction project, for which the blueprints must be highly specified and must remain pretty stable. In software it's usually pretty straightforward to remove a chunk of code during the course of execution; in contrast, it's not so simple for a construction project to remove, say, an entire floor that's already been built.

4) Is the customer willing and able to offer flexibility on scope?

We ask this because Agile defaults to scope buffers to help manage project risk—specifically, the part of the product backlog comprised of "nice-to-have" features, as opposed to the "must-have's." If things go wrong and you're only able to deliver on the must-have's, then the project is still successful, even if only minimally so. If things go well and you're able to deliver on the entire product backlog, then you will have exceeded customer expectations; but this only works if the customer is willing and able to offer flexibility on scope. If they don't stipulate any "nice-to-have" features, or are unwilling to pay for them, then the scope flexibility that Agile requires simply won't be there.

If all four of these questions can be answered affirmatively, then Agile—and especially Ultimate Scrum—will likely be your most effective choice of project delivery methodology. It is important to note, however, that Ultimate Scrum is designed to rely more on schedule buffers, in contrast with most Agile/Scrum approaches, so if using an Agile/Scrum approach that is schedule-buffered, Question #4 will be less relevant. In addition, we should note that, while Lean Process VSAs serve as a highly effective companion to Ultimate Scrum, they can complement any approach for software-enabling business processes.

CPSIA information can be obtained at www.ICGtesting.com
Printed in the USA
BVOW11s1706020615

402806BV00001B/2/P